NASTASSIA C.S.

I0505854

THE ~~PERFECT~~ ~~PERFECT~~ PERFECT LAUNCH PLAN

HOW TO GET OUT OF YOUR OWN WAY SO YOU CAN FINALLY START A BUSINESS
(EVEN WHILE BUILDING A FAMILY)

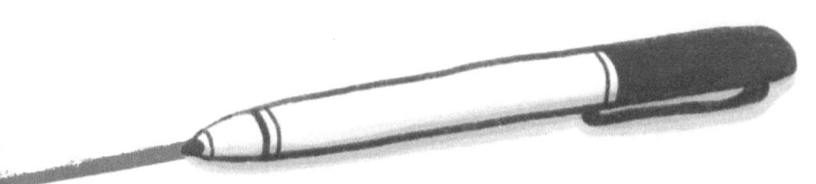

ISBN-13: 9798633732290

ISBN-10: 1477123456

Library of Congress Control Number: 2018675309

Printed in the United States of America

Contents

Introduction

Not long before my thirteenth birthday, I moved to the United States with my family. At that age, while contending with all the changes happening in my body and my mind, I had to learn and adapt to the American culture as well as navigate the immigrant journey. Like many immigrants before me, I began to fully realize and experience my otherness. The way people looked at me, their expectations of me, the way they spoke to me, and the way I was treated seemed to me, even at that age, to be very different. It was also the first time I had people — and most shockingly to me, the American education system — point out to me that I was a brown person, and it didn't take long for me to get the message that brown people were perceived as inferior. So at a time when my world was already being turned on its head and I had to enter a new school (brutal at that age), learn a new language, adapt to a new culture and customs, I was also thrust into a new identity that immediately made me less than others.

It probably comes as no surprise, then, that in order to adapt, my instinct was to make myself as invisible as I could. So just as most of my peers were starting to explore, experiment, and begin the process of discovering who they were, I was going the opposite direction. Wearing the right clothes, speaking the right way, getting the right grades, pursuing the right interests; not standing out too much in any way became my survival tactic. In the process I missed the opportunity to develop an identity outside of what others told me I should be. The result was a messy couple of decades where I made a lot of mistakes and developed into a person who was outwardly confident and strong, yet deeply insecure and unsure of myself. I constantly questioned my authenticity, not knowing which parts of me came from within me and which were a product of my effort to conform to other's ideas of "good," "normal," and "cool." One thing, however, always remained a constant: I knew I was an entrepreneur. I had the ideas, the desire, and the hunger, and I knew how to brush off a failure and bounce back ready to pursue the next thing.

By the time I reached my 30s I had failed multiple times at entrepreneurship, and had quit more jobs than I could count in my quest for control of my professional narrative. The beautiful thing, however, is that by this time I had also done years of self-reflection, identity exploration, and could finally look myself in the mirror and see a person who I could forgive, love, and encourage. Fortunately, it was not until I felt this sureness in who I was that I became pregnant.

Gestating, birthing, and parenting is a wild experience. I love my child, and I love seeing myself grow as a person through parenting, but I am not a person who "found my purpose" after becoming a mother. Parenting is a side of me, but having struggled to form my identity, I set boundaries for myself and continue to grow and explore who I am outside my role as a mother and partner. Becoming a parent did force me to rearrange my life and reset my values, and it solidified the idea that I had to make entrepreneurship work. So with a growing belly and a deadline, I promised myself that by the time I had my baby, I would have a thriving business. I spent my pregnancy building something of my own so I could avoid going back to the corporate world, and while my body was busy making a baby, my mind gave birth to two successful ventures, completely changing my life and my idea of what success looks like. Today I run a consulting firm, and most recently launched a business incubator for women founders.

Having worked in Silicon Beach on and off for a decade, my first instinct when starting a business was to seek out the help of an incubator. Why wouldn't I want to make sure I had what I needed to succeed by getting support and help from experts in the beginning stages of my business? I had a hard time finding an incubator that fit my new lifestyle and was willing to help me in the ways I really needed, however. Most wanted a business to be pretty far along in their launch, almost all were in a large city, requiring easy access to a major metropolitan hub, and to be accepted, a founder had to be willing to be physically present for the duration of the program, typically 3 to 6 months. In addition to the impossibility of leaving a newborn to take part in a 3-month program 6 hours away, I doubted there would be support dealing with the uncertainty of parenthood, sleepless babies, breastfeeding, and all the other challenges a new parent faces as they are getting ready to launch a business. More than that, these incubators were focused on the business journey, not the emotional journey that entrepreneurship really is.

Being a natural entrepreneur, I immediately saw an opportunity in the gaps. So as I grew my consulting business and navigated parenthood, I took note of my steps, strategies, hacks, wins, losses, and most importantly, the mental hurdles I had to overcome along the way. I knew I was not alone in the quest for flexibility, financial independence, freedom, fulfillment and fun in the complicated journey of launching a business. Furthermore, I knew intimately the doubts, fears and insecurities I had to overcome along the way before I could allow myself to become the CEO and mother I am today. These lessons eventually became the foundation of my incubator, through which I guide women all over the world through their business launch, their mindset shifts, their self-empowerment, and yes, parenting.

The more I learned from the women I coached, the more I had the desire to make the information I shared with them available and accessible to other women and mothers with entrepreneurial dreams. I wanted to reach even more people who were being held back by their own insecurities. That inspiration became this book.

While writing, I felt like I was writing for myself. I wrote it to the person I was before, who no matter how many business guides I read, could not find a single one written by someone who looked like me, who spoke about how freaking scary it is for someone full of baggage to start a business. This is not just a touchy feely self-help book, however. I offer you real steps you can take to go from desire to launch.

This book is broken down into chapters that address each of the major steps most entrepreneurs take in the business launch journey. Each chapter closes with a "mental breakdown" section to address some of the most common mental challenges you are likely to face as you progress. I opened these spaces for you as a respite from the go go go nature of entrepreneurship. These are fears and insecurities that I have personally experienced, and that I see the founders in the incubator go through regularly. My hope is that you gain some insight into overcoming them and feel comforted knowing you are not alone. I encourage you to be honest with yourself. Allow yourself the time to feel these emotions and tackle these fears, and even if you can't identify with some of it at the moment, read through each section so that if they do come up for you at a later stage in your journey, you have the tools to identify and process what you are going through. I have also given you permission slips to think, feel, and do the things a lot of us tend struggle with. Don't be afraid to tear them out of the book (in fact, I encourage it) and tape them to your bathroom mirror, glue them to your vision boards, or post them on your refrigerator so you have constant reminders of your power.

It is my hope to be as inclusive as possible, so I want to make you aware of the few assumptions I make regarding what you have available as you embark on this new venture. I assume you have access to: internet, some startup capital, a willingness to learn, and a commitment to growth. And although this is a "how to" guide, I don't want you to see the order as a rule. Read it once, take note of what's applicable to you, and feel free to follow whatever flow makes the most sense for your business. So get ready to get ready, and let's dive in.

Allow yourself to be great,

Nas

Chapter 1

Bulking Up Your Mental Muscles

T o celebrate my life partner's birthday and the fact that I had recently quit a cushy but soul-crushing job, we went on a road trip through Northern Mexico. We made our way through wine country, stopped at beautiful beaches, and I had timed it so that on our way back to the U.S. I could meet with a business coach (who I could no longer afford) to try to figure out exactly how the hell I was going to pull off starting a business without the safety net of an income.

The day before we were set to cross the border and make our way back to the U.S., my instinct told me to head to the nearest pharmacy and get a pregnancy test.

Yup, I was pregnant.

Suddenly, meeting with a business coach felt a lot more urgent. Before our trip I had decided there was no way I would ever go back to the corporate world with my tail between my legs, begging to go into a cold office every day, to do a job I had no passion for. Not only did I have that promise to uphold, I was now also unhireable.

I had known for years that the standard corporate lifestyle wasn't for me, yet I let so many fears drive me back time and time again. But now with a whole new set of fears, and a new human on the way, I no longer had the choice to fall back on my old patterns. You see, I have a history, a cycle if you will:

1. Get a job
2. Get miserable
3. Have genius business idea
4. Quit job
5. Start business
6. Fail miserably
7. Repeat

This 7-step process is something I have repeated countless times since I was a teen. By the time I found out I was pregnant I had grown tired of it, and done enough growing up to know that this time failing was not an option I wanted to entertain. I was sure I knew the "right" steps for starting a business, and I knew that the problem wasn't my ideas, so what exactly was keeping me stuck in that loop?

Never in any of my previous attempts at starting a business had I taken the time to think about my mental state before and during my journey. Standing at a distance now, I can easily see all the fears, insecurities, and traumas that were holding me back. Yet in all the books and guides I read, the workshops I took and the research I did, I never had someone stress the importance of massaging and exercising my mental muscles before starting a business — at least not in a way that connected with me and my experience. I never had a coach or mentor who could relate to being an immigrant, a person of color, the years of conditioning I had been through to become a "nice girl," or how childhood trauma, shame, or low self-esteem could hold someone back as an entrepreneur.

So if you've ever failed at running a successful business or you've ever been too afraid to start, let me tell you what I wish someone had taken the time to tell me: You have to be VERY mentally strong, and you have to start bulking up those mental muscles way before you actually make any forward motion in starting your business. I certainly don't mean that you can't run a business if you are a sensitive person. In fact I wish we had more sensitivity and emotional support in business settings. But I am saying that if you are not prepared to face some of your deeper fears, they will get in your way sooner or later in your entrepreneurial journey.

At this point you may be thinking, "Do I really have to unpack all my shit before I start a business?" Of course not, that work takes a lifetime. You need to start making room for this work as soon as possible, however, because when you hit the point in your business where your initial momentum and excitement wanes, it'll be a lot easier to keep going if you already know yourself well enough to recognize where the lull is coming from.

To help you in that process, throughout this book I help you identify the most common insecurities, fears, and doubts that show up during each stage of starting a business. In my work as a business coach for women and mothers, I have seen repeatedly that when people can name what they are going through and feel less alone in those feelings, overcoming them becomes less of a challenge. So let's dive in.

Fear of Failure

This bugger has roots in so many areas of our lives, but the most common place this fear comes from is the idea that as women, either we achieve perfection or we are complete failures. We tend to leave very little room for being good enough as we are. I have worked with women who are simply paralyzed when it comes to putting themselves out there and launching their business, unless everything is absolutely perfect — which it never is — and they know for sure that they'll succeed. So they end up planning and planning and then planning some more, only to find themselves 2 years into starting a business without having actually done anything.

For me, fear of failure would manifest in me doing only 90% of everything. I would go super hard, do all the research, put in a ton of work, build the foundation of something great, and then... abandon things at the last minute or in the final stretch. I was so afraid of failing that pushing through to the end of things meant that I never really had to put myself out there and risk failing in the first place. Of course, this meant that I also never gave myself a chance to succeed.

The thing to understand here, however, is that fear of failure doesn't actually have anything to do with failing. It's all about shame. And shame has a way of worming its way into your brain until you find yourself coming up with spectacular ways to sabotage your happiness.

Ironically, all the ways I found to avoid shame — lying, glossing over important details, running away and avoiding problems —put me in a deeper spiral of shame that I suppressed; never coming clean, never being truly honest with people trying to help. This is what shame does. It makes you feel so low and think so badly of yourself that you forget the truth: Failure comes from a set of actions you can learn and grow from, it does NOT represent who you are as a person. In other words, failing is an action, not a state of being.

Whether you have seen fear of failure pop up here and there in your life, or you consider it a close friend, exploring where your shame comes from so you can find ways to let go of it, will help you tremendously in your startup journey. Because if there is any universal truth about entrepreneurship, it is that you *will* fail. And the sooner you can start seeing failures as opportunities and actually get excited about them, the higher your chances of succeeding will be.

Because no one was there to give me this advice, I jumped in head first and now have an ego full of scars and broken relationships to prove it. I left my mom, who was my business partner at the time, to close out our failing business alone; I went from excellent credit to the depths of debt; I ruined the relationship with my most recent business partner and one of my closest friends. And when I actually began to do the work of uncovering where my shame came from so I could understand why I had done so much damage to myself, to others, and to my failed businesses, something else began to surface: Annoyance. Annoyance that every single thing – everything – came down to abuse I survived as a child. How cliche is that!? It had been like being in a maze where every time I hit a dead-end and turned back to try a different path, I would hit the same exact dead-end. For me, that dead end was the after affects of a history of sexual abuse.

Having been molested by my grandfather and then told to lie about it, coupled with being a naturally sensitive person, I formed a belief that I should be ashamed and secretive of who I am. And because of that false belief, I would do anything feasible to keep my shortcomings from surfacing. Whenever I felt confusion, overwhelm, or when I felt I had made a mistake, asking for help or forgiveness would never even cross my mind, as it meant that others would have to be aware of my failures. And as much as I'd like to avoid filling this book with overused theories, everything truly is connected. Whatever limiting belief you hold in your personal life, it will show up in your business at one point or another, so nip that shit in the bud now.

It was only through working to uncover the origins of my limiting beliefs that I was able to understand my shame (and trust me, it was not an overnight turnaround). My willingness to connect the dots between that early abuse and my behavior patterns, made it so much easier to see my roadblocks as necessary steps in my path to growth, rather than proof that I was the terrible person I had made myself out to be. So as you start to do this work, remember: be kind to yourself. Treat yourself with compassion and understand that whatever your rate of growth, that's the right speed for you. No one can overcome trauma or let go of deep-seated beliefs on a schedule.

Fear of Success

Now if you read the previous passage and are like, "Ooff, what a doozy!", let me tell you about Fear of Failure's big sister, Fear of Success. Now that you know that fears can – and often do – come from shame, it's easy to see how fear of success would also come from a similar place. To be clear, people who experience this rarely actually fear being successful. It's more about what happens when success does come and insecurity around what success might bring. If you come from little money, this fear can manifest in insecurity around not knowing what you would do if all of a sudden you had a ton of it. If you were always ridiculed for doing well when you were a kid, you probably learned how to hide your accomplishments. Alternatively, If you were taught to make yourself small and unnoticeable, then the exposure that might come with success probably wouldn't sound like a desirable thing to you.

The way this little jackass showed up for me was in the form of imposter syndrome. I had this ability to see myself moving on from failure and trying again, but when I tried to see myself really succeeding, all that came to mind was "Will I know how to manage all that money?"; "Do I have enough knowledge or experience to help others?"; "Will I know how to hire a team and train them?"; "Can I really be a boss, someone responsible for people's income?"

That's the thing you will also notice with fear of success. Even though you have a desire to start a business and be successful at it, you may find it difficult to picture yourself there or anticipate the positive feelings that come with fulfilling your dreams. So what can you do about it?

Focus Wheel

Allow yourself to celebrate where you are now and let each win propel you to the next one. One exercise I like to do whenever I am feeling a disconnect between my big goal and where I am in the present moment is a focus wheel. For this, all you need is a piece of paper and time.

To set up your focus wheel, start by writing the wish you want to fulfill in the middle of the page. For example: "I am a wealthy and happy entrepreneur." If you are not there yet, this will feel like a reach. That's the point. Then start surrounding that statement with things that *are* true for you that lead back to your center statement, e.g. "I love learning about entrepreneurship," "I really like my business idea," or, "I know there are people out there who will also love this idea." On and on. You want to surround that reach statement with phrases you can say out loud and feel in your gut that you know are true for you in this moment.

The point of this exercise is to make that big statement less daunting and less anxiety-filled by attaching it to things that make you feel good and hopeful. And since fear of success can be just as a paralyzing as fear of failure, you want to adopt practices that take you away from fear and anxiety and into hope and excitement.

Fears in the Context of Parenthood

Fears and insecurities will be active partners in your business. Add being a parent to that mix and it can be enough to freak anyone out. Imagine fear of failure with a dash of "I am not a good enough parent," or fear of success with a big dose of "if my business really grows, I won't have time for my kids." I see a lot of people in my line of work try to convince me that because their fears are coming from a place of caring for their kids, that they are somehow different. But I don't buy it. Sure, as parents, we have sets of fears and insecurities that others might not, but they all stem from the same place. I also happen to think that making your kids responsible for you holding yourself back not only places a heavy burden on them, it also teaches them that personal dreams and desires can wait. So to do this work and really transform yourself into an entrepreneur, you have to be willing to own your fears without adding the mask of parenting in order to allow yourself to grow.

Making Peace with Growth

The reason why I name these fears right in the beginning is to help you see that, while doubts and insecurities will be partners in your business, growth and learning need to be your co-founders. Decide right now that you will do everything in your power to use every roadblock as a step up to the next win. To put it simply, you have to adopt a growth mindset before you can jump into anything that requires perseverance. Leave no room for self deprecation or a defeatist attitude in your journey to becoming a business owner.

If you have any doubt that believing you can learn and improve has more value than whatever you think about your abilities, look into the journeys of the people you admire and I guarantee you will find stories of people with a strong belief in growth and personal change. And if you are still a skeptic, I recommend you look into the work of Carol S. Dweck, author of Mindset: The New Psychology of Success. In it, she defines a growth mindset as the belief that one can learn and improve, and its opposite, a fixed mindset as a belief that skills and intelligence are fixed qualities that we either possess or not. Unsurprisingly, people with a growth mindset are better equipped to succeed in areas where people with fixed mindsets tend to fail. The biggest benefit to adopting this way of thinking is that you can always make the choice to move from fixed to growth when you catch yourself believing that you "can't" do something.

Mental Roadblocks

So you've decided to adopt a growth mindset and you're committed to finding a lesson in every challenge. Cool, you are fixed now!

Obviously that is not how it works. Just as I can guarantee you'll have challenges you can learn from in your journey, I can also say with certainty that no matter how committed you are to growing and learning, there will be days you will want to quit. There might even be days you wonder why the hell you decided to do this in the first place. That is also part of the journey.

Me, I love the beginnings of things. In the beginning you are full of passion, enthusiasm, optimism, and momentum. In the beginning, you haven't yet learned all the things you didn't account for, and you are in a constant state of blissful ignorance. Then, the middle comes. It could be a few months or a few years into your journey. One day, you will be lying in bed at the end of a long day thinking of ways to escape. I can tell you that at least once a month I fantasize about starting another business from scratch or dropping it all to start an Etsy shop.

So what do you do when this happens to you? First take the time to acknowledge that this is completely normal. Then, instead of immediately pushing that thought aside, actually take the time to look at what's causing you to feel that way before you make any decisions. If you can identify a specific fear surfacing, exhaustion at the end of a particularly long day, the need for some time off, an interaction with a difficult client, or anything else that you can find a solution for, you know that this is a problem that can be solved and a barrier you can overcome. Now, if you have racked your brain and it looks like there is no way out and that continuing would make you miserable, it might be time to actually scrap the whole thing and find something else to do.

Wait, what? Am I really, in Chapter 1, telling you to quit? Yup. It is really important that you hear this right at the beginning. Starting a business is about making your life better. You are doing this to bring something you are currently missing into your life. So if at any point you start to feel like there is no part of you that sees the positive in what you are doing, I give you permission to quit.

This Is Not a Hobby

There are so many reasons people start the businesses they do. You might be finally starting work on something you've been passionate about, but don't have experience in, or you could be taking years of learning in your industry and applying them to create something of your own. Regardless, the one thing I ask of you is that you don't call this your "side hustle." Either start a business or start a side hustle. Sure, you may have known people who turned their "side hustles" into full time jobs, but telling yourself right at the beginning that what you are starting is a "side" thing strikes me as another way we tend to minimize our efforts and our worth. Telling people — and yourself — that you are doing something on the side shows a lack of commitment, a lack of seriousness, and a lack of belief in your own ambitions. Ouch, that's harsh... and most likely not true, but I totally get it that it's easier to skirt around fear of failure if you don't make it seem like you're really trying to make this a proper, prosperous business. So unless you really just want this to be something you do on the side, stand tall and proud when you tell people you are starting a business.

The easiest way to start to feel like an entrepreneur is to adopt the identity of an entrepreneur. So rather than thinking of this as a hobby next time someone asks you "what do you do?," take a breath, and try this out: "I'm an entrepreneur and I'm in the process of launching a business at the moment." Actually, put the book down right now and go say that to yourself in front of the mirror. Go on.

How did that feel? Awesome? Badass? Scary? Fake? Whatever that felt like for you, it's totally okay. This exercise is all about helping you get comfortable in your new definition of yourself: that of a true entrepreneur. Someone on a mission to grow an idea into a business.

PERMISSION SLIP:

YOU'RE ALLOWED TO WANT MORE

Chapter 2

Family Matters

I hear a version of the following from mothers I coach on an almost daily basis:

"I was going to do that, but there was so much family stuff going on, I just didn't have time." And every single time I hear this, it's always on the heels of a challenging phase in their business launch journey. Yes, being a parent, especially the parent who is responsible for the emotional labor or the household administration, makes starting a business that much harder. I get that, I really do. What I also get is that as you continue working to develop your entrepreneur identity, you will have to shake things up at home and reset others' expectations so you can set yourself up for success.

If you have a life partner or other people with whom you share domestic responsibilities, it is crucial that you set expectations and boundaries for how this new venture will fit into your lives. The easiest way to do this is to schedule a time to sit down and have a purposeful conversation. The goal is to negotiate space for your business obligations so they don't create tension or unforeseen disruptions in your home life.

I remember being so annoyed when I was starting a manufacturing business because my life partner at the time would walk in and out of my work space, talking on the phone, making noise, talking to me, and generally being distracting. After hours or even days of this behavior, I would burst at him with an annoyed, "Can you stop doing that!? I'm working here"! But could you really blame him? I had never actually told him that a) I had designated a part of our living room as my new headquarters, b) that between the hours of 10am - 4pm, I expected to be able to work from that space, or c) that I needed to not be disturbed during those hours. I expected him to not only read my mind, but also be completely okay with me taking over a large part of our living space for the majority of the day.

Let me veer off for just a bit here... What my lack of respect for our shared space actually showed went much deeper than just a lack of communication. At that point in our relationship the amount of resentment that I had let accumulate was so out of control that I'm surprised we were even talking at all. At that time, I was also pretty depressed, lost, and scared shitless of failing in my business (spoiler: I did). Looking back now, because I had not taken the time to fully prepare my self mentally for what I was embarking on, and did not have a good support system at home, it was no surprise that I attracted exactly what I feared: Failure.

Now, back to the topic of setting expectations. The best way to prepare for a conversation with the people who make up your support system is to first think about all the ways your routine is about to change. Then show up to the conversation with solutions and a flexible mindset in case something doesn't completely align with others' availability or capability. Some things to think about are:

- How will this change your physical space?
- Will you be using part of the house that is now serving another purpose?
- Where will those activities be moved to when you are working?
- How will this impact everyday life?
- What hours in a day and days in a week do you plan on dedicating to your business?
- How will this change your current availability at home?

- What are your expectations of those around you when you are working?
- What are the ways you will need extra help?
- Who will provide that extra help?
- What about finances?
- Have you talked about whether you will be using your shared funds in your business?
- Will this change how much you contribute to the household?
- What will change in your child care needs?
- Will you need to change pick up and drop off schedules?
- How will your availability for childcare change when you are at home but working?
- How will you create boundaries for the kids?
- Who will be responsible for enforcing them and how?
- Will you need to add an after school activity to open up more time?
- Who will be responsible for figuring that out?

This may seem like overkill, but trust me, it's much easier to adjust to a new dynamic when everyone has an idea of what to expect ahead of time. This will not be the only conversation you will have around yours and everyone else's expectations for how things will change once you dedicate yourself to starting a business. But this first talk sets the stage for how you and your partner should approach the changes. Rather than having a screaming match about how sick they are of hearing you say "I'm here, but I am *working*!" you can put 20 minutes on the calendar to sit down again to voice concerns and come up with new solutions.

My current (and amazing) partner and I had to sit down for one of these "State of the Union" talks after our recent move, and three years into my latest venture. Everything was running smoothly, and he and I were completely clear on boundaries, but I was noticing that since the move I was taking care of a larger percentage of household management tasks, which was starting to get in the way of my business. So I asked for a time to talk, let him know the topic ahead of time (division of household tasks), and together we came up with a great compromise that neither of us was too ecstatic about, but were willing to agree on for the sake of the union. It was agreed that I would continue to take care of those tasks because he was still working on learning the language of the country we had recently moved to, and he would take care of all the cooking.

It's also good to note that you can and should prepare the setting for these conversations to bring you joy, so that both of you start associating these chats with something fun. Pop a bottle of champagne, whip out a pint of ice-cream, plan a picnic, go for a hike together or plan to go to a movie after. Whatever works to get you both in the mood for a talk.

Unleash Your Selfish Side

I used to constantly run into situations where I would say yes or decide to just do something myself simply because I was conditioned to "be nice" to others. I would realize halfway through a task that I was doing something I didn't necessarily want to do in order to avoid making others uncomfortable by insisting they do their fair share.

The expectation that some of us place on ourselves to please others, make others comfortable, constantly be available, and always be aware of others needs, is so ingrained, that we hardly even notice how often we appease without considering our own opinions and feelings.

It wasn't until recently that I confronted my mother and stepfather to let them know how inconsiderate they had been to ask me, as a very young child, to be responsible for fostering the relationship with my stepfather when he came into my life. By constantly asking me to "be nice" to him, "go say hi" to him, and generally make sure that his feelings weren't hurt when I was just being my shy self, I was being taught that no matter what *my* feelings were, making sure others felt good was my priority.

Your entrepreneurial path will be filled with instances where you have to stand your ground and be able to say no. Every new vendor and contractor you hire, every new sample or asset you have to approve, and every request for meetings can be triggering, and you run the risk of quickly finding yourself floundering and unable to set appropriate boundaries. Think back about the messaging you got throughout your life. Where and when were you encouraged to say yes, be nice, or put other's feelings before your own? You don't have to do a deep dive, but you want to start noticing the things that trigger this behavior in you.

I have met a few women in my lifetime that don't share this trait or instinct, and if you are one of them, congratulations. But for the rest of us, it takes a lot of work and self reflection to be able to slowly move towards a place where we feel entitled and deserving of our own time.

When starting my journey as an entrepreneur, the thing that felt most counterintuitive was realizing that now that I had a baby and a dream of starting a business, it was time to learn how to focus on myself. When it came time to tell my partner that I would need him to earn the money or take care of the baby while I worked, or even to do the dishes and cook so I could have time to get things done, just thinking about the conversation filled me with guilt.

As you get ready to embark on this entrepreneurship journey, it is imperative that you find your "selfish" side. Because what happens to people who are constantly doing things for others is that they keep giving and giving, and when people aren't as appreciative as expected or available as desired, they become resentful and angry. And those emotions don't help you as a business owner, a parent, or partner.

I still often find myself saying "yes, I'll run that errand" or "yes, I can take a few minutes out of my scheduled work time to listen to your problems and ideas," but I now can easily recognize if that's coming from a place of trying to please people or if I truly feel like I want to be of assistance in that moment. You want to be able to make this distinction because there will be a thousand and one ways that others' need will seem more important than your own, and when it comes to reasons why I've seen women fail they own businesses "I had to help [insert other person here]" is high up on the list. So allow yourself to let go of all the negative connotations the word selfish may bring up for you, stake your selfish flag on the ground, and wave it proudly.

You Can Work It Out

I want you to think about what you see when you picture an "entrepreneur." Does the word conjure up images of amazing suits, walk and talk meetings, power poses? I know that's what I had in mind the first time I launched a business. And sure, I love a good excuse to wear an amazing power outfit, but the reality is that when you are starting out, your day to day will probably look pretty different from what you picture.

If you have a tendency to seek perfection in everything you do, this is the time to start letting go of some of the notions you have about what entrepreneurship will look like. The sooner you can get cozy with the idea that things will not be exactly as you picture them, the easier you'll be able to move beyond hurdles and find opportunities where others would see obstacles.

When I decided to start a business when my baby was only 4 moths old, I organized my days to fit around naps and feed times, but as any parent knows, naps are tricky devils and just when I thought I'd be able to step into a meeting, I would hear that lovely little cry that signaled it was Mom Time. But because I had created my business to work around my life and not the other way around, because I had set expectations and boundaries with my colleagues and clients, and because I had let myself be okay with the fact that I had chosen to be a working mom, showing up to a meeting a with baby hanging off my boob was just part of doing business with me. Even as I was prepping to write this book, I had my kid on my lap constantly taking away my pen and demanding belly kisses, and for me, that's exactly why I started a business to begin with. To be able to enjoy these moments and have this seamless transition between life and "work."

There will be countless ways that your non-business life will make its way into your business, and that can be a beautiful thing. Knowing that you can always find a flow – if not a balance – between the two is what makes this journey worth embarking on in the first place.

Business Schminess (Adding Fun Back Into Your Life)

Now that you have your partner on board, your life organized, and you've made the choice to prioritize your business, let's get to work.

Hold up. Not so fast.

There will be times when your new business stresses you out, and even the most zen of us can spiral into tunnel vision and forget that we are embarking on this journey to make our lives better. Every single one of the mothers I have coached mentioned having more flexibility and freedom as a goal when starting their business. Initially they talk about these things as some far off goal post, something that will come when "x" thing happens for them in their business. But guess what? You can – and should – start adding those things into your life right now. It is extremely important that you prioritize flexibility, freedom *and* fun right at the beginning. By baking the freedom you crave into the core of your business, you not only get to immediately reap the benefits of entrepreneurship, but also avoid having to reshape your business when you are at full steam. So ago head and add free time to your calendar alongside your work hours.

After all, your family can be the perfect antidote to a stressful meeting, a lost client, or a delay from a vendor.

Let me show you what this can look like in practice. I know that since my kid doesn't go to school until 1:30 in the afternoon, I have to be flexible when it comes to what I can schedule in the mornings, so most days 8am - 1pm is set as Morning Family Time in my calendar. During that time, we go for walks on the beach as a family, play, ride bikes... we make memories, we have fun. And that is just as big a priority in my calendar as any meeting.

Later in the book I get into more specifics around scheduling and finding time for your business even if you have a busy life. But for now, as you start to fill your calendar with work tasks, make sure you also schedule and prioritize "family time," "fun time," and "me time." This may seem a little too structured for some, but just seeing those in your calendar helps you see them for what they are: the things you said you'd have more time for once you started your own business.

You are About to Give Birth... Again

Remember the first time you became a parent and all of a sudden you became *that* person? Constantly talking about your baby and your parenting experiences as if you were the first person to ever have a child. Well, get ready to go through it again. Because if you are starting a business that you are passionate about (and if you are not, go back to the drawing board), it'll change your life in many of the same ways that a first child does. A new business demands a lot of attention and can keep you up at night when ideas tend to pop into your head. You may have a clear vision for how you will run your business and how it'll grow, but suddenly it starts to develop a personality of its own and all plans and projections go out the window. And just as we have constant doubts about whether we're doing the right things for our kids, you'll often wonder if you are making the right choices in your business.

If you are lucky, after a while you start to relax and realize that yes, you will make mistakes, but as long as you keep showing up and doing the best you can, things will turn out okay. So when you encounter times that make you think you are not cut out for entrepreneurship, just think of it as parenting: no matter what happens, you can't decide that you won't be a parent anymore, but you can make the choice of what kind of parent you want to be. So make the choice to become an entrepreneur and decide what kind of entrepreneur you want to be every day.

Mental Breakdown: Guilt

As soon as I started to write the session on unleashing your selfish side I could hear all my Supermom friends... *what do you MEAN you are telling people to be selfish? I don't think I would even know how to do that! If something comes up, OF COURSE I am a mother first.* And on and on. You can be someone who truly finds yourself after you have a child, and discover you are completely fulfilled in the role of full-time care giver, but for those of us with ambitions in addition to parenthood, dipping into the pool of guilt is a near daily occurrence.

As you start to open room in your life for your new venture, you will notice that guilt will find ways to sneak into those spaces when you least expect. Guilt might crop up when you choose your business over your family and friends. Or when you choose your family over an important networking event. When you find yourself thinking about work during family time, or realize you actually would rather be fleshing out that cool new idea than playing with your kids. You may even find that you feel guilty about having waited so long to do something for yourself.

Regardless of how it shows up for you, it doesn't serve you. I used to think that my guilt meant that I cared. I'd stay up freaking out about all kinds of things I wasn't doing, Googling at all hours of the night, just so I could find a way to "fix" whatever it was I felt guilty about. Or worse, I'd obsess over an issue and think of a thousand ways I could have done things better. That's when I realized that it wasn't about guilt at all. All these bad feelings stemmed from some ancient passed down belief that I had to be perfect: Be everything for everyone all the time, and look good doing it. So I would use guilt as a way to torture myself for falling short of perfection. That's pretty whacked out!

Guess what? You *can't* be everywhere at once and you *can't* be everything to everyone. And you sure as hell cannot be perfect. What you can do is keep building a version of yourself that feels good to you at this moment — and feel free to change this as often as you need. If being an entrepreneur is part of that vision, accept right now that at times your business will come first, at times your family will come first, and some times (and I am strong believer in adding more time to this bucket), _you_ will come first.

The whole point of doing this, of embarking on this crazy journey, is to make life better for you and those around you. Walking around feeling guilty all the time does not make you a better person and it will not make you a good entrepreneur. Let go of guilt and be your sloppy, spacey, and sometimes, smelly self.

PERMISSION SLIP:

YOU DON'T NEED TO HOLD ON TO GUILT

Chapter 3

Set Yourself Up For Success

Y ou can start a business without any of the things laid out in this chapter. I've certainly tried to, but why would you? The whole point of this book is to make starting a business not just stress free, but actually fun. I want you to be psyched every day. Not just about your future success, but about where you are at this moment.

A quick note before I jump into the practical: Whatever your reason for wanting to start a business, I find that most people start with the idea that "when x happens, I will be so happy!" The secret to a good life, however, is the exact opposite. When you make the shift to simply being happy right now, positive things start to happen. Yes, some of you will look at this statement and think it's some law of attraction mumbo jumbo, but my question to you is: Even if you don't believe that positive thoughts bring positive things, what's the harm in appreciating where you are right now?

This chapter is not just about setting yourself up mentally. Here you will find lots of practical tools to make fitting your business into your life a lot less complicated, without a ton of effort — so good!

Meditation + Exercise

If you haven't been convinced by now that we should all be meditating daily, let me be one more person to tell you that yes, you should be meditating. If you have any doubt about the power of meditation, I direct you to the millions of search results that come up when you look up "benefits of meditation." Personally, I can't live without a consistent meditation practice because it gives me a safe place to go in my mind whenever I feel anxiety trying to take over. Not only that, I now crave the deliberate tech break, the freedom of letting myself do absolutely nothing for a few minutes, and the chance it gives me to allow new ideas to pop up.

Creating a space of a few minutes every day when you can slow down, disconnect, and look inward is one of the best things you can do for yourself. However many people still have a hard time getting themselves to that place where their mind is calm. So how do you mediate when your mind just won't quit?

First, let go of the idea of "clearing your mind," which can leave you feeling like you are "not doing it right." Instead, set a goal of unplugging first and create a space where you will be free from most distractions. Notice I don't say *all* distractions, not only is that hard to accomplish, once you get the hang of things, you will find that, like me, even with a toddler running around it is still possible to meditate. So even if your space is not a zen garden, as long as you can stop your phone from ringing, you are doing good. Then set a timer, and just chill. Close your eyes if you want, keep them open if that works best for you. Now you want to start to pay attention to the boring things around you. The traffic noises outside, a buzz from an air conditioner, a singing two-year old. And let yourself stay there for as long as you can. When thoughts start to come into your mind, acknowledge them, and silently tell them "Thanks for showing up, but I'll see you later, I'm busy now." Do that for 5, 10, 15 minutes every day and soon you will start to notice the difference between the days when you do meditate and when you don't. If you prefer something more structured like a guided meditation, or want to escape the everyday sounds around you with a pair of headphones, a quick online search for "meditation apps" will yield hundreds of options. Remember, this is *your* daily ritual, so try as many as it takes until you find the one that works for you. When I started, I downloaded the most popular app because it seemed to work for everyone but when the narrator's voice started to annoy the hell out of me, I downloaded and tried at least 5 other apps until I settled on one that had a timer and coffee shop sounds, which for some reason worked well for me [insert shrug emoji here].

If you *really* cannot stand the idea of sitting quietly for a few minutes, I recommend you at least find a soothing breathing exercise you can quickly perform in the moments you find yourself feeling anxious. One that works really well for me is to breathe in deeply for a count of 4, hold your breath for a count of 4, and breath out slowly through your mouth until you've let all the air out. I then repeat this as many times as needed to bring me back to a state of calm. The beautiful thing about a meditation practice is that it helps bring order to the chaos that our minds become when we are thinking of the endless tasks we have to accomplish for our businesses, while simultaneously setting up a school pickup and jotting down a grocery list.

Physical exercise on the other hand builds so many skills you will need on a daily basis and it also gives you space to release built up stress. When you carve out time to develop a consistent exercise routine, you are taking the time to build your stamina, your sense of discipline, as well as creating yet another opportunity for meditation. When you are in the zone while exercising you are freeing your mind, and you may find that some of your best creative thinking will happen during this time. I know that this can be difficult to add to an already packed scheduled, so if you really cannot fit in a 20-minute workout a couple of times a week to your agenda, try to find opportunities to multi-task or split your activities. I have seen clients couple phone meetings with long walks, or break up 30 minutes workouts into 3 10-minute breaks throughout the day. Sometimes clichés have it right, where there is a will, there is a way.

Time Management

The number one reason people come to me for help with launching their business is lack of time, or more accurately, lack of time management skills. A lot of people subscribe to the prevailing belief that you can either work 8 hours a day for someone else or 16 hours a day for yourself, and they wonder how they can start and grow a business when life demands so much of their time. I definitely had this mindset in my first attempts at launching businesses. I would fill my days with endless tasks and stay up until all hours of the night finishing projects, prepping, or researching. It wasn't long before I realized that when I broke things down, I was barely making $5 an hour, and I was actually busier and more overwhelmed than before. So all that freedom that I wanted to bring into my life as an entrepreneur was nowhere near becoming a reality.

By the time I was launching my consulting firm as a new mom, I thought "why not start with the freedom I want *now* and fit my business in around my ideal work schedule?" And I realized that if I was going to be my own boss, I wanted to be a really flexible, understanding, nurturing, patient, and cool boss. So the first thing I did was sit down with a day planner and fit in all my home life tasks in the appropriate time slots. Here's a sample of an average day:

6:00am - Wake up

6:15am - Meditate and journal

7:45am - Morning family time [breakfast + play + family walk]

11:00am - Nap

1:00pm - Lunch

1:30pm - Day care drop off

6:00pm - Day care pick up

6:30pm - Dinner

7:00pm - BBB [bath, book, bedtime for baby]

Once I could see what my day looked like with home life filled in, then I could start to fit work in *around* my life without compromises. So what this looks like for me is this: around 11am, when I put my kid down for a nap, I know I can do some business tasks that don't require a whole lot of planning, like checking emails and going over my to-dos for the day, in case he wakes up early. Then when he is in daycare I can fit in everything else that requires a solid commitment like meetings, coaching sessions, and general management of my businesses. I also don't schedule anything for the evenings because I find that I am just not productive at the end of the day, so I usually save them for reading, relaxing, and connecting with my partner.

As you can see, my actual work day fluctuates from 4 to 5 hours, and I most definitely don't get every single thing done that I could in a day. What this means is that my business perhaps doesn't grow as fast as some others, I can't take on as many clients, and sometimes people have to wait a bit longer to schedule a meeting with me. But every day when I write "morning family time" in my planner, I still smile in pure gratitude knowing what a gift it is to have that time. I feel incredibly blessed that I get to wake up with my family, play with them in the morning, have lunch and dinner together, and that I get to be there for nearly every BBB (bath, book, bed) time.

Obviously, not every day can be planned and not every business allows for every single thing to happen on your time. But this exercise very clearly shows you what time you do have available so you can start using your time more wisely. I have the luxury of 4 uninterrupted hours a day, but you may have only 30 minutes in the morning and an hour in the afternoon — what can you do in those times that will truly move your business forward?

After you figure out exactly how much time you have in a day, the next step is to write down the 3 things you want to accomplish daily. That's it, only three things. Knowing exactly how much time you have allows you to be more realistic with your to-do. Learning to prioritize your tasks will also help you move forward more quickly and see more consistent results. You will also find that having less on your to-do list and actually crossing things off at the end of each day will keep you way more motivated than a massive to-do that never seems to get smaller. Before I had a kid and had all the time in the world, I could work work work and frequently accomplish nothing. Once my time became more limited, I learned how to use it more effectively.

It's about doing more with less and really taking advantage of the resources you do have, rather than complaining about what's missing. What I want you to see here is that the best thing you can do when it comes to time management is to shift your mindset from "I don't have any time" to "How can I make the best use of the time I do have?" See the difference? One is a fixed mindset that you can't do anything about, the other lets you find the opportunity so you can have the freedom you crave now, not later.

Once you've organized your time and have a goal for what you will accomplish each day, the real time management work begins. While prioritization gets easier with practice, knowing how to focus on the task at hand in the time you have allotted can be a challenge. Sure, you have set aside 30 minutes to work, but if you jump to check your phone as soon it buzzes, or decide that first you need to clean the house, you will lose some of that time you set aside for yourself and your business.

I definitely struggle with focus and my biggest challenge when I first started was my environment. I would set aside my work time, but would find myself picking up dishes around the house, organizing my workspace, and generally tidying things up around me before each work session. For me, these were things that were easy to focus on because they gave me a clear sense of accomplishment — cleaning the dishes has a definite start and end — whereas in my business, each task leads to another task that leads to another task after that. This meant that, instead of working for the 45 minutes I had in between things, I really only had about 30 minutes.

So how can you get in the zone and focus on your priorities in the time you have? First you want to start by clearing your workspace from distractions. Put your phone in another room, turn it off if you can. Resolve to set a scheduled time for cleaning the house, or delegate that task. Block the most distracting websites from your browsers (this literally changed my life). Make sure you are wearing comfortable clothes. Go to the bathroom. Grab a glass of water. Grab a snack. The trick is to think of yourself as a 4 year-old and make sure you remove any "shiny balls" from your workspace.

If your work involves a lot of time in front of a computer, like mine does, then using that technology to your advantage makes a lot of sense. In this case, you can start by setting a timer. Sometimes just knowing the clock is ticking is enough. For me, though, I had to go one step further and find ways to turn off the outside world. Right before I start my timer, I put on a good pair of headphones and search YouTube for "focus music." If you want to invest in a focus app, there are some great ones out there like focus@will, which matches your personality to music that will make you more productive and focused, and includes a timer. Over time you will discover what truly gets you in the zone and what slows you down. This knowledge will speed up the process of getting into "work mode."

Be gentle with yourself in the process of discovering what works. It took me a while to figure out that while I really like jazz, it doesn't work well at keeping me focused for an hour at a time, and even though I love having my long-distance meetings at home, going to a co-working office space works much better for me when I need to focus on administrative tasks. Feel free to create a work flow that truly works for you. After all, part of the reason we crave leaving our 9-5 is having the freedom to do things our way. The thing most people don't realize, however, is that freedom sometimes has to be crafted and well thought out — otherwise we will just continue following the same patterns we developed in our day jobs.

Education

I like to start my business coaching engagements by asking founders what they see as their biggest personal obstacles to launching a business. Lack of knowledge is by far the number one response. I love hearing this because it is an easy obstacle to overcome and because we are so lucky to be surrounded by resources nowadays. While we will dive deeper into good investments versus bad in Chapter 9, I would like to skip ahead a little here and assure you that acquiring knowledge is one of the best investments you can make for your business.

You will quickly see that as a founder, you will have to wear many, if not all, hats in the beginning, so the more you know about all aspects of your business, the better you will be able to delegate and hire later on. Even if you think you will never be the one doing your financials, marketing, design, copywriting, or sales, knowing at least the basics of every aspect of your business will make you a more informed leader who will make better choices.

The best part about this process is that for most people, it can be very organic. Instead of wasting a ton of time trying to learn everything and delaying the start of your business, you can invest in your learning as your business progresses and new skills are needed. And though I see education as an investment, it does not mean that you have to spend a lot of money on learning.

A great place to start is your local library, an asset most people overlook. While there is a lot of good content online and YouTube can basically provide you a college education nowadays, the library is a great resource because it can be very well curated and give you access to information that you would otherwise have to pay for. The best part is that a lot of libraries now also have digital content, so if going to a physical library doesn't fit into your schedule, look into whether your local library has a partnership with a digital content provider. What this usually means is that you can borrow the hot new book on marketing, or investment, or crowdfunding from the comfort of your home and not feel like you are stuck because of something you don't know. When in doubt, get yourself a book.

Put Your Own Mask First

Just as exercise and meditation will help you build the stamina to grow a business, there are two very important things you want to make sure you have accounted for that will help prevent burnout and stress.

First, as you work on your schedule and begin your new time management routines, you want to make sure you find space to pencil in self care. Think of self care as the thing that instantly creates a better, more relaxed mood. It could be a manicure, a walk in the woods, a massage, a night out with your friends, 3 uninterrupted hours in front of the tv, sex... whatever it is, make sure to add it to your weekly schedule and make a promise to yourself to keep that appointment no matter what happens. In entrepreneurship, there is plenty of room for stress and if you start to lose yourself in your business, you run the risk of resenting the time you spend on it, which will only lead to more burnout and stress.

The other really important thing to have in place when you switch from a 9-5 to full time entrepreneurship, is health insurance. Technically this does fall under self-care, but because it doesn't sound as sexy as a massage, a lot of business gurus tend to skip over this advice. Maybe you are lucky enough to live in a civilized place that offers quality healthcare for all, but for a lot of people, especially parents, foregoing good health insurance can put you and your family at a huge risk. So pretty please when you are going over your financial plans, and allocating where you will invest your money, make sure good health insurance is on the top of that list.

Mental Breakdown: Perfectionism Masking as Progress

You may find that even though you are setting realistic time management goals, the feeling that you are not doing enough might start to creep up. I see so many people stumble when they start to equate being busy with being productive.

What I often see in the founders I work with is a tendency in the beginning of our time together to want to fill any available time, including late nights or early mornings, with random to-dos that don't actually move their businesses forward. Worse, they become excuses to keep their businesses stuck. I have seen people get fixated on their logo and branding, spending hours and hours on design and delaying their launch for when everything looks amazing. Others get obsessed with research and wanting to know every single thing there is to know about some aspect of their business, delaying their launch for when they know it all. In my case, I felt like I had to set up every tech tool in the world, including things that I clearly didn't need yet, delaying my launch for when "everything" was in place.

We tell ourselves that we are doing the right things for our businesses, and complain about how much work we are doing and how busy we are. No matter what you decide to stay busy with, however, the root of the issue is always the same. In the end, what we're dealing with is perfectionism, plain and simple.

Of all the mental hurdles I consistently help my clients through, the idea that as women we have to be perfect is the one that seeps into most areas of our lives. When I stopped to think about all the ways that I, a progressive feminist, still find myself striving for perfection, I was shocked. Through subtle actions and self-talk, I still see myself as someone who should have the perfect body, be the perfect wife, perfect mother, with perfect hair, who's perfectly dressed, and is a perfect coach, perfect writer, perfect leader, perfect daughter... Fuck! The worst part is that I'm not conscious of most of it.

There's no way in hell I can or even want to be perfect at all those things. Because I have been taking care of my relationship with myself for a long time, when I notice these patterns reemerging, I can quickly take a breath, realign, get back on track, and allow myself to just be me, knowing that perfection is not only impossible, it's also boring. Yet here and there I still catch myself looking at everything that I am and finding ways to tell myself I am falling short. But when it comes to moving a business forward, done is always better than perfect. After all, you are starting a business to change your life money, so every time you get stuck in perfection mode, you are getting in the way of that goal.

The best way to get ahead of this, at least when it comes to your business, is to practice the time management tools I've shared here, so that you can become aware of how you are actually spending your time. So if you notice yourself start to spiral down the path of seeking perfection, feeling like you are "busy" all the time, losing focus on what matters, telling yourself that what you are doing has meaning, yet you see no actual progress... stop and ask yourself: How is this task moving my business forward? Or how is it interfering with forward momentum and keeping me from what I really want? Answering these questions honestly will bring back perspective and set you back on track.

PERMISSION SLIP:

YOU DON'T HAVE TO (OR WANT TO) BE PERFECT

Chapter 4

Painting Your Business Picture

When I am interviewing new founders who want to join my incubator, I always ask them this question: Imagine you've been accepted and everything works out exactly as you want it to, what does your life and business look like one year from now? The answers usually fall somewhere along the lines of "Everything is up and running and I have consistent income and profit" and "I have more freedom to do what I want with my time". Then when I push a little further and ask for specifics, what does your day-to-day look like, how many people have you hired, what's your daily routine, what are you doing with your newfound free time, people get a little less certain, if not downright stuck. What surprises me about this is that though people say they are ready for a change, they find it difficult or never actually think about what that change looks like. In other words, people often know what they don't want, but have hard time allowing themselves to picture and imagine what they do want.

When people start businesses without determining a set of values and without a clear picture of how they want to structure their new venture, they very quickly start falling into the same traps that got them to the stressed out state they were are fleeing from when they decided to be their own bosses. Meaning, when you operate on auto-pilot, letting prior experience, other people's businesses, antiquated ideas, and the status quo, guide how you will build your business, you are setting yourself up for stress and burnout down the road.

I remember distinctly telling my then friend and future business partner that I was done working for other people who frustrated me, and that I rather work harder for myself than half-ass it daily for someone else. We decided to go into business together and because I was operating under the assumption that working for myself regardless of what I was doing was enough for me, I failed to fully analyze what I was getting into. I never stopped to think that if when this business succeeded, it would actually fit the idea of success that I had in mind.

We ended up starting a manufacturing business of kids products, and I very quickly fell into a pattern of work that consisted of a combination of research, marketing, administrative tasks, design, business development, sales, delivery, and pick up of goods. I was also working (i.e. staying busy) around 14 hours a day, six to seven days a week in an industry I knew little about and had no connection to (at the time I had no kids and ultimately did not know my ideal clients' needs very well). After a little over a year of this, I was exhausted, burned out, lost, depressed, and I was once again in the same spot I had been before I started the business: knowing what I didn't want because I had failed to define what I wanted. This happens every day. People go into business for themselves because they crave freedom and while they find freedom from having a boss, they give up so many other freedoms along the way simply because they failed to define their wants. To get ahead of this, you can start by defining what success looks like for you.

After we shut down operations on our kids business, I was still 100% sure that I had to continue on as an entrepreneur, and by my next venture, I was able to turn all the items on my "do not want" list into a set of values and a business operation guide for myself. My intention for this chapter is to help you avoid all the time and money it took for me to realize that just starting a business is not enough. I will walk you through the process of creating a set of values for your future business that will help you guide your day-to-day operations, so you can continue to be as excited about your business 3, 5, 10, 20 years from now as you are about it today.

You Get to Define Success

To define how you'll be able to create a business that truly brings you the freedom and joy that you crave, you have to be willing to let yourself think for and about yourself, your business idea, your hopes and your dreams in an honest way. Take me for example, if I had stopped to write down my own values and desires before I decided to go into manufacturing, it would have looked something like this: passion, environmental consciousness, working 1:1 with people, short work days, opportunity for business travel, deeper understanding of the human mind, emotional development, and ample vacation time. Looking at this list now, it's a wonder I lasted as long as I did in manufacturing. It's obvious looking at it from the perspective I have now, that I was working directly against my values. I didn't have much passion since I didn't really understand our customers, therefore I didn't really understand our product. I was working on making new things thereby creating a business that was wasteful and a huge contributor to pollution. I hardly had any opportunity for working with people one on one. My days were definitely not short. There was some travel, so that was a plus. But there was no room to apply my desire to better understand the human mind and watch people develop emotionally when customer interaction was brief and mostly virtual. And to top it off, vacation was tough because there really is no break in manufacturing. It should have been obvious that I was going into the wrong line of business, but when you are lost in the excitement of starting something yourself, it can be easy to let yourself think this is what you really want.

Now let's take a look at how my current business operates:

I am incredibly passionate about diversifying people's idea of what a successful business founder looks like. On most days, my business creates little to no waste. I work around 4 days a week for up to 4 hours. I work with people one on one, on a daily basis. I travel constantly to meet with clients and for pleasure. I have clients with whom I have been working for years, and have had the privilege to witness their emotional, mental and leadership development growth up close. And between living beachfront on a beautiful island and being able to bring my work anywhere, so I can travel with my family, I feel like I am on a constant vacation.

The only difference between finding success in one business versus the other, is the time I took to plan how my business was going to operate by looking at my values before I got started. Had I had a different set of values, I could have succeeded in manufacturing and failed at consulting and coaching. With each set of values, comes a different idea of what success looks like. Had I been successful in manufacturing, that success probably would have looked like having a big production of our products, being sold in many stores, which would require a lot of employees to handle sales, delivery, online operations, in a big office with standard departments like marketing, customer support, engineering, design, and so on. My workdays would probably be pretty hectic, filled with strategy meetings, sales updates, quarterly goals and quality control. This would also mean that we would be invested in continually growing our business year over year, bringing in investors to help us scale. Ideally, we would have expanded our product line and eventually become a big player in the kids clothing and gifts industry. I would probably be making a lot of money as a co-founder of a large business, and would likely have to continue on as CEO or COO to ensure our steady growth. Looking at it from an outsider's perspective, yes, this does look like success. Anyone who starts a manufacturing business and is passionate about making it work, hopes that this will be the trajectory of their business. But when you look a little closer, you can see the details and in those details is where you will find your values... or not.

To achieve this kind of growth, I would have to be very involved in the day-to-day of the business, I would have to like the power and responsibility that comes with being a CEO and I would have to enjoy or see value in seeing my products being sold everywhere. I would likely keep a pretty set schedule, my days would be filled with meetings, having an office from where we could operate would also make things easier, and I would definitely have to be in it for the long term. While none of these are negative to owning a business, in fact can be quite attractive to some, they just don't align with who I am and my own business values.

To avoid finding yourself in the middle of something which doesn't align with who you are, when you start to think about your values, it will be helpful to let your definition of success guide you. And to help you define what success looks like to you, start to think about what the ideal version of your business looks like on a day-to-day basis:

- What time do you wake up?
- Where do you go to do your work?
- What's your commute like?
- Who do you see when you walk in your office?
- What tasks fill your day?
- Do you envision a bustling headquarters?
- A quiet private space?
- What title do you hold?
- What thoughts, feelings and ideas does your brand conjure in your clients mind?
- When are you finished with work for the day?
- How many people do you employ?
- How long do you see your self in this business?

Since by now you have started to structure your calendar, find a 20-minute slot in your day and allow yourself that time to sit and define the values that are unique to you when it comes to the business you envision yourself founding and growing. Feel free to use the questions above as a jumping off point.

As you do this, make sure to spot anything that could go counter to the business you currently have planned and ask yourself if these are things you are willing to compromise on or if it's an opportunity to come up with a creative solution to aligning your values with your vision.

Question Everything

As you start to bring the vision you have of yourself as a founder closer to the reality of running an actual business, it's time to question the status quo.

Sure I ultimately may have not been passionate about running a manufacturing business, but had I not been stuck on the idea that manufacturing had to contribute to pollution, I could probably have adjusted my business model so that it did suit me and my idea of success. What I mean by this is that you have complete freedom to create something new. Just because most manufacturing businesses operate a certain way, it did not mean that mine had to follow suit. *This* is your chance to create something completely custom to you, that works for you, and attracts the right kind of people whose vision also aligns with yours, be them customers or employees.

A lot of the ways we consider to be standard in how businesses operate were put in place at a time when values were different, social norms were different, and people's general idea of success was very different. If your goal is to create a massive company that employs thousands, you don't have to have a 5 day, 9-5 work schedule for everyone. If your idea is to start something that allows you to work from home by yourself, it doesn't mean that you can't achieve massive growth. It wasn't that long ago that the idea of a company with a completely remote workforce seemed crazy, if not impossible. In fact, there are people who still think it's not possible today, even as the number of remote only or remote first organizations keeps growing. Nowadays organizations are also seeing massive gains by shortening the work week from 5 to 4 days and implementing other strategies to help improve the balance between work and life. We now also have lactation rooms in offices, paternity and maternity leave policies, unlimited Paid Time Off policies, and a number of other ways organizations are changing how they operate to provide everyone with a better quality of life. And while I recognize that it might seem like a needless exercise to think of operations of a large scale business when you might still be in the idea phase, allowing yourself the chance to question and challenge the status quo, can give you the freedom to think bigger, better and smarter about the future of your business.

When I think back now, had I allowed myself this freedom, I could have been a pioneer in pollution-free carbon-neutral manufacturing. I could have structured my business in a way that allowed me the freedom I have now, and still achieved the growth necessary to keep a business like that running. But because I was basing my business on others that had come before mine, using their strategy for growth as a guide to mine, even though it went so against my values, I set myself up for failure from the beginning.

I am lucky that I had the perseverance and resilience to eventually find my own way to this freedom based thinking which ultimately led me to starting a business where operations run according to my own standards. And by asking you to start questioning the status quo now, my hope for you is that you get to skip the heartbreak of having to shut down a business because it fails to bring you everything you want. I also hope you find the courage and confidence to create a business that will bring you all the joy, fulfillment, freedom, security, pride, and time that you envision for yourself, while also making space for your future employees to experience the same passion you feel about your business.

Design Your Culture

How exactly can you manage to create a business that fulfills your needs as well as those of your future team? From the countless organizations I have worked with, I can tell you that the culture is very much dependent on its founders and how they choose to operate in the early months and years.

As the founder of your business, it falls on you to define what is rewarded, and what is not tolerated. So being thoughtful and deliberate now, will save you from having to try to stop a moving train later on. And while the early days of a business can be filled with uncertainty, having a clear guide will make the hiring of your early team much easier and transparent. In today's work environment, people are looking for more than just another job. They want to know that whatever organization they join is a place where they can find purpose, fulfillment and alignment with their own values. Hiring can be a time-consuming and expensive process, so making sure your early hires see long-term potential for themselves will not only save you time and money, it'll help solidify the culture as you choose to define it.

The simplest way to define a culture when you are in the beginning stages of your business is to define your company values. Just as you defined your own personal values so that you could create a business that is suited for you, you now have the chance to think about how your business will operate so you can create an organizational culture that attracts the right kind of people to join your team, as well as provide transparency for your customers on what kind of business they are choosing to invest in. To help you get started, here are some questions you should ask yourself as you start to define your company values:

- Would you like a competitive or collaborative work environment?
- How important is innovative thinking?
- Will you have a hierarchical structure?
- How do you hope to promote a healthy work-life flow?
- When you have the means, what types of accommodations and benefits can people, especially those with families, expect?
- What are the expectations of a new hire in their first day? Month? Year?
- What will motivate people to show up every day?
- What kinds of behaviors will be rewarded?
- How will people be recognized for their wins?
- How will failure be handled?
- How often and in what format should people expect feedback?

- How will professional growth and development be promoted?
- Are there any environmental practices that your organization wants to adhere to?
- How do you define the social impact of your business?
- Is there a charitable component to your operations? If so, what and why?

Just as you set up your 20-minute timer to define your personal values, you want to do the same thing here, keeping in mind that the goal of this exercise is to paint a clear picture of what it'll look and feel like to work at your organization.

Diversity, Equity, and Inclusion

Now that you are thinking about the future of your business and realizing that eventually, this new venture will also impact the lives of all of those who choose to join your team, it's a good time to start thinking about where you stand when it comes to valuing diversity, providing equitable access to growth for all, and what how to encourage inclusivity in your day-to-day operations.

Let's start with diversity. It has been proven over and over again that organizations with a diverse workforce fare better than those that don't, so I won't spend any time making a business case for it. However, one thing we do tend to overlook is what diversity means. Sure, it can mean diversity of race, gender, sexual orientation, and physical ability and you should absolutely strive to create a workforce diverse in those ways. But beyond that, diversity should include social economic backgrounds, education, employment history, culture, and other ways you can think of to bring as many varied thoughts and perspectives to your organization. This is the kind of diversity that will help your business in the long run. To create a better product, reach a new customer base, understand pitfalls, diversity of thought will be your best bet.

From my work as a diversity, equity and inclusion consultant, I would say that diversity is the easiest out of the three to solve for because when it comes to equity and inclusivity, we often can't see past our own biases. That's because being inclusive requires empathy and most people think it's hard to be empathetic to everyone when they're trying to grow a business. In reality, it is just another part of your product and sales strategy: providing everyone on your team an equal chance to grow and feel like part of the culture will directly contribute to the improvement of what you are all creating. So when you think about performance ratings and opportunities for growth in your company, remember that equity and inclusion can only be achieved when you have already made diversity of thought a priority.

Hiring

It is true that in the beginning you do get caught up in just getting the business going and it might be a while before you have to think about culture, DEI (diversity, equity and inclusion) and hiring. But it is very rare that a business is able to grow consistently without a little bit of help. So if that means hiring an assistant to help you with the administrative stuff, signing a contract with a long-term vendor, finding a designer, a marketing specialist or a strategist, hiring decisions will come sooner than you think.

This process will already be made easier if you have your company values defined. But if this is your first time hiring someone how do you know if you are making the right choice?

Back when I first started my search for an assistant, I was so desperate for help that I just hired the first person who seemed like a good fit from a quick interview. I had needed someone to help me with responding to inquiries via social media, scheduling, organization, as well as someone who could help manage my ad campaigns. To get her trained, I set up daily calls, shared spreadsheets of tasks, signed up for a great software service to help us keep track of different projects... Basically, I thought I was doing everything right to make sure that her and I were working well. After all, during her interview she had talked about how organized she was, and how comfortable she was with new technology. Fast-forward to six weeks later, and when I tell her I'm confused about why things are progressing so slowly, that I haven't seen her update our project tracker, and that I see unanswered questions from possible clients in the system, she lets slip that she hates social media, and that she'd rather track things on her own. What? I had just wasted so much time briefing her on my business model, my strategies, her role and expectations and *now* she was telling me that she "wasn't in to" the basic tasks required for her job!? Obviously, we didn't work together for much longer, and I was upset at myself for not having been more through in my search, the interview, and relaying exactly what her job description would be, and most of all I was annoyed that I would have to start the search all over again.

Unfortunately, this scenario is quite common. I still see big corporations that I work with today make the same mistakes. They have a hiring process that is supposed to guarantee that new employees are qualified and are a good fit for the role, but ultimately everyone agrees that some times you just don't get it right. The difference is that these corporations can afford to keep searching for that perfect match, whereas when you decide to make your first hire, you will likely be in a place where you need to fill the role yesterday. When your business grows past the point where you are not able to handle everything, there's no time to read 78 resumes, interview 35 people, do a reference check for the 13 that you think might be a good fit, and still have time to train your new hire.

After that experience, I started to look around and research more efficient ways to making a hire when you are pressed for time. What I found is that because my business is so closely related to emotions, feelings, empathy and a love for people, I needed to bring all of that to my hiring process. I also learned that I needed to play to their strengths, so that instead of trying to find an assistant to do everything, I could offer part-time positions to multiple people and find people who were absolutely psyched to only do things that they were passionate about.

Essentially what I discovered was that if I was creating a business that was changing my life for the better in ways that were specific to me and my wants and needs, why not do the same for my employees? This meant that I could hire a mom who would rather homeschool and play wither her kids all day, to help with Customer Support at night. And that I could find an ad campaign management genius who likes to work with multiple clients, instead of trying to teach ad management to someone who would rather organize my schedule in her free mornings. So instead of making one bad hire, I can make three awesome hires who now get to run their schedules in ways that work for them, as well as for me and my business. Can you can say win-win-win-win?

The other great learning that came from this new strategy is that as with everything else, you get to run the hiring process in any way that works for you. Instead of relying on the same old processes that you had to go through when you were hired for a job, you get to make the hiring journey for your company as interesting and as fun as you want. I now like to use a few personality tests as well as creative questions in my application process. I have seen people use numerology and astrology, riddles and tests as part of their hiring process. Essentially, as long as your process is fair and gives people equal chance to show you their strengths and capabilities, you absolutely should make this an enjoyable part of your business. The only rule here is that you are looking for people who can be passionate about your company values, and commit to giving, as much as they hope to gain from working with you.

Digging Deeper Into Operations

Earlier in this chapter, I briefly talked about operations and how you might want to run your business on a day-to-day basis. I also encouraged you to start questioning why most businesses operate so similarly to one another. Now we can take a deeper look into organizations that chose a different path, so you can start to brainstorm how you would like to eventually structure your business.

We can start by looking at ROWEs or Results Only Work Environment. This business operating model is actually pretty simple and if you are starting small, easy to implement from the beginning. Essentially, a ROWE works based on the premise that if you give people a clear understanding of what their goal and objectives are, and give them the freedom to achieve those in whatever way works best for them, you will have a much more motivated and productive workforce. In a ROWE, each individual understands that they are part of a team, but they are not tied to having to be at their desks, miss family events, or work insane hours to prove as much. The belief here is that as long as your work is getting done, go ahead and take the afternoon off to go to your kid's soccer game.

One model I strongly believe in is the 4-hour workday. Back when I was still working 9-5, I remember the moments in the day when I would open a new browser window to randomly surf the internet, or the 6 trips to the kitchen snack cupboard, and the multiple times I would check my phone throughout the day. If you were to add it all up, I can confidently say that my best work was done in about 4 hours, leaving the rest of the day to random tasks and general time-wasting. In those 4 hours, I was actually going above and beyond what was expected and consistently hits and surpassed my goals. So it wasn't that I was unmotivated, it's just that the nature of what I was doing didn't requite me to be at my desk for 8 hours. And it wasn't just me, there were lots of people working beside me whose job didn't take all day, but because the structure of our days were mandated by the corporate structure, so many people were unmotivated to truly give it their all. I even tried to bring this up to one of my bosses, but my advice fell on deaf ears. What I realized however was that I wasn't alone. I heard from so many people that if they had the chance to have less time at work, the improvement in their quality of life would be a huge motivator for increasing their performance and productivity. I'm also a big advocate for a shorter day because I truly believe that technology is supposed to make our lives better. If you have the ability to be reachable, there's no reason you have to be in an office all day, when you can email with your colleagues to resolve a work issue when you are at home.

If freedom from a traditional office environment is something you are looking for, you can also set your business up to be remote-first or remote-only work environments. As the name suggests, this means that you prioritize people working remotely which means you either have a small headquarters with the majority of your employees working remotely or that you don't have an office at all, allowing you to find talent anywhere in the country or the world when the time comes for you to make your first hires. Remote-only work places do require a great deal of discipline as each person has to be self-motivated and it also requires some planning, thought and effort to make sure everyone remains engaged and supported.

These are just a few examples of the ways you can choose to run your business when the time comes to make new hires, and while it may be hard to think that far ahead in the future, these are the kinds of decisions you can start to make now so that when the time comes, you already have a crystal clear picture of how your organization will operate. And remember, this is fun. You are the boss and you literally get to say what goes. You get to reinvent how a business can grow, be successful, while still making sure that everyone involved gets to enjoy the work they are doing and hours they are putting in to make your dream a reality.

Mental Breakdown: It's Just Me

So you just finished this chapter and now you may be thinking "whoa, wait a minute, I just want to know how I can start a business, so I can make my life a little better. Why is she talking about how I want to run a corporation!?" And yes, I get that going from "I want to start a business" to "think about how you'll hire your future employees" might seem like a big jump, but I want to sell you on your bigness right from the beginning. Even if you end up being a one person operation, make sure that it's by choice, not because of fear. No matter your business idea, it does have the potential to grow beyond what you may even be allowing yourself to dream right now.

Even today I still get a pang of fear when I think about my business growing beyond a few people. It's not that I don't think my business doesn't have the potential, but it's the idea that I may not have what it takes to effectively run a large scale operation. Like I am somehow not educated enough, not smart enough, and just not the right person for the job. But I am experienced enough to know that is just my lizard brain trying to run the show.

You will definitely run into situations when you feel like the leap from where you are now to full-blown CEO may seem insurmountable. During these moments remember that although it is perfectly normal to feel this fear and to feel like you are not enough, these thoughts are coming from a part of your brain that is trying to protect you from failure and disappointment. And even if it feels like that part of your brain is right, I want to you embrace the fact that you are going into this *hoping* to make mistakes, and excited to learn from the failures along the way. You have heard basically every successful CEO echo this sentiment about failure for a reason. We, humans along with listening way too much to our lizard brain, also tend to forget that we never truly learn from words, only through experience.

So get cozy with failure, get excited about feeling scared shitless when reaching for more than you think you can, and get psyched to do things you've never done before.

PERMISSION SLIP:

YOU ARE FREE
TO RUN YOUR
BUSINESS SO
THAT IT
WORKS FOR
YOU, NOT
AGAINST YOU

Chapter 5

Test, Test, Test!

L et's get down to business, shall we? We now finally get to dive into the problem you will be solving by starting a business.

A lot of people who come to me for help do come up with an amazing idea from a life experience, but they just as often come to me with an entrepreneurial desire, and no clue as to what kind of business they intend to run. So to begin, let's take a look at how you can set a spark of inspiration and come up with a business idea that is worth your time and effort.

Live In the Future

To conjure up a truly great business idea, you want to find ways to ignite your imagination. The easiest way to do this is to start paying really close attention to your life and the details of your day-to-day. When you commit to looking at your life through the lens of someone who wants to solve problems, you start to see opportunity everywhere. You can start to make it a game to notice all the little ways that your life could be improved by something that either isn't available yet, or could be improved upon. Ideally, you want to start a business that will fill a gap in your and other's lives. I know that as a parent, I usually think of at least 10 things that could make my life easier, before breakfast, and while not all of them have the potential to be great businesses (like a biological clock regulator for toddlers), I like to write them down or speak them out loud to my partner to keep my idea machine well oiled. Remember, no problem is too small to solve and a great idea can come from anywhere, so don't be so quick to dismiss what comes to you. Write it down and set a time to come back to it later to analyze if that idea seems like something you might want to dedicate some time to.

Let's say you like to surf or mountain bike, but you don't own a car and don't live that close to the beach or a mountain. Next time you notice yourself struggling to find a friend who can help you lug all your gear, you think "hey, it would be really cool to be able to order a ride that had a rack and plenty of storage space, so I could just pack my things, get to my destination, practice my sport and then order a ride back without having to worry about parking or cleaning up." Bam! You now have the seed of an awesome business idea: A ride sharing service exclusively for outdoor sports enthusiasts.

You see, you don't have to come up with some ingenious never before seen idea. Improving on already existing products or services might actually be a better route for you as a beginner, since the basic concept has already been proven to be a success.

Once you have a few ideas you feel confident about, the next logical step is to check these ideas and their basic concepts against your personal values. I am not seriously going to consider starting another manufacturing business that uses plastic or cheap labor because it goes against my values of environmental preservation and human rights for all. But for someone else, coming up with an amazing product that uses plastic but will dramatically improve the lives of others might be a no-brainer. Compromising on your values just to start a business because you think it'll make money, never works out in the long term. You may well make a lot of money, but emotionally and psychologically, you are setting yourself up for disapointment. When in doubt, always go with what looks like it'll be most fun!

Once you have narrowed down your ideas to the ones that will solve a real existing problem and gel with you on a deep level, it's time to share it with those who matter.

Research, Research, Research

While a lot of people still start businesses based solely on an idea without ever reaching out to their ideal audience prior to launching, I beg you not to go down that path. First, it's a huge gamble that may or may not pay off, secondly, you will spend way more money shifting to what your clients want later on, so go to the source before you start throwing money around.

The first serious business I started was a boutique that showcased up-and-coming international designers. I would meticulously source and buy from up and coming designers from places like Brazil, Colombia and Spain. The shop itself was charming, the designs were carefully hand-picked, and the price point was ideal for people who valued investing in unique, quality pieces. To me, this idea sounded amazing. I mean, I would shop there! So why was it that only a couple of years later, we had to shut our doors?

I never got out of my head before embarking on this venture. The only perspective I had was mine. So it should have come as no surprise that when we opened our doors in a neighborhood filled mostly with young college kids without a ton of disposable income or occasions to wear luxury clothing, we didn't exactly attract the swarm of people we thought we would. If I had just taken my time to survey the people walking around that area about what kind of store they felt was missing, or if I had done some more research into what part of town would have had more interest in my concept, I probably would have done things very differently based on that feedback. Instead, I spent a ton of money on inventory, setting up the store, and paying rent before I had any idea if others would connect with what I was bringing them.

You would think that after that experience I would have learned and done a ton of research before jumping into another business. Instead, I made that same mistake two more times before I started to believe in research. So if you think you have the most amazing idea, you know it's going to work and everyone will love it, you want to start your business as soon as possible, but the only opinion you are basing that on is either your own, your friend, your kid, your uncle, whoever... you might want to give it another thought.

I get why people feel leery of research. So many people still believe that if you run around sharing your idea with other people, someone might steal it and there goes your genius flash of inspiration. But here's the truth. It takes a lot of work to start a business, so even if someone thinks your idea is worth stealing, they are not likely to start that business tomorrow, so you can chill out a little bit. And if they do end up stealing your idea, great. They just saved you a lot of money and time. The other reason I have heard people use is that they don't want to share their concept and hear negative responses. I totally get it. You are already putting yourself way out there by admitting you seriously want to start something on your own, and sharing an idea that you may be unsure about, the last thing you want to hear is that people hate it. But the cool thing about getting out of your head and talking to people, is that even if someone thinks it is the dumbest idea they have ever heard, there is so much juicy stuff you can learn from this kind of negative feedback. Do they hate it because they are not the right audience? Do they have any suggestions that might improve your original idea? Can they think of anyone that would benefit from your service or product?

You see, what you are actually doing by surveying people is letting *them* build your product for you. When you talk to enough people, you start to see trends in your responses and from there you can build something specifically for the right audience and market. This way you will never have to wonder *if* people want what you have to offer, it'll simply become a matter of *how* to reach them.

After you have become intimately aware of what your ideal customer wants and you have a better idea of what your product and service will be and do, you can start to look at your competitors. Because once you know for a fact that there is a need for what you want to offer, what people want to see in your product or service, and the pain points you will be solving for your ideal customer, you can bet there is someone out there who is already doing something at least similar to what you are doing. Your job is to become as familiar with how they are doing things as you possibly can. You want to make sure that you take note of everything they are doing right, and how you can improve in the areas where they either are failing or have chosen not to invest in.

Just look at the current products available for women's periods. Now we have period panties, menstruation cups you can use while having sex, organic cotton reusable pads, customizable home-delivered tampon boxes, and even though all these businesses essentially do the same thing, they each have a product that is marketed for a specific woman. But it wasn't that long ago, that our options were pretty limited, uncomfortable and generally not very effective. What happened? How did we start a menstruation revolution?

All it took was for several people, mostly women in this case, to start to notice that what was available was not good enough and to pick up where the competition was falling short. So as you start to refine your idea, there will be no better guide than your competition.

When I decided that I would start an incubator for mothers who wanted to bring more freedom into their lives through entrepreneurship, the first step I took was to ask the women I was already working with — and lots and lots of strangers — if this was something they were looking for. First I let them tell me exactly what they were missing when it came to starting a business on their own, and how they envisioned getting the help they needed. Once I saw that underrepresented women with little time and little business experience had a huge need for a step-by-step guide to starting a business from someone like them who understood motherhood and the mental hurdles needed to succeed, I started to study what was currently out there for them.

Coming from a startup background, I was already somewhat familiar with the landscape. But still, after doing more research, I noticed that yes, there were incubators trying to reach a more diverse demographic of founders, but even these were still following practices set in place by older incubator models that made it almost impossible for a mother with young kids to get the kind of support one needs when starting a company. All the reputable incubators I studied required a lengthy process of application and approval, a minimum amount of business know how and experience, proximity to a large metropolitan area, ability to participate full-time in the program during regular business hours for a minimum of three months, and most required that founders give up a percentage of the company.

Now imagine you are a mother raising a toddler and a baby in a small town, already working full-time, who has a business idea, but no experience... even if you find the time to go through the application process, there is no way you are going to be able to leave your kids for three months to go to a big city and take part in an incubator. And that is the gap I sought to fill.

Can you see how the seedling of an idea can turn into a fleshed out business model through research?My initial intent was to help women be better business leaders, but it was only after surveying my audience and studying my competition —

and before I spent a single dollar — that I could paint a complete picture of what my offering would be: a fully remote incubator program, that would welcome all levels of experience, cater to those short on time, offer a safe space to tackle the emotional hurdles of entrepreneurship and motherhood, and wouldn't require a stake of the founder's businesses.

For people with experience in business this process of validating your idea may seem like a no-brainer, and is better known as a Proof of Concept, but when you are just starting out and you don't know what you don't know (like me before my first business), we have to start with the basics.

Proof of Concept

I have given a high-level view what a Proof of Concept can look like, but my goal is to fill this book with as many specific steps as I can, so that you can have the confidence and knowledge to take real steps forward in your business. Assuming that you are starting from scratch, have no social media presence, and would rather not spend a bunch of money, there are a couple of options for how you can run your proof of concept.

Option #1: Survey

This is my preferred method of proving a concept because it gets you talking to the people who will eventually become your customers right away. The first thing you want to do is come up with a simple set of questions that will help you understand people's desire for what you have to offer, the features they would like to see, if and how much they would pay for your product, and most importantly what pain points would be solved by your product or service. Here are some sample questions that you can customize according to your idea:

- What's your current situation with [problem your ideal will solve]?
- What would you like your situation to be instead?
- Why is that important to you?
- What's getting in the way of you getting [the result they want]?
- How have you tried/what have you used to solve this problem so far?
- What are the top 3 things you worry about when you think about [problem]?
- What would be the top 3 benefits to [solving this problem]? How would your life [looks/career/social impact/income] change?

* Are there any influencers, brands or publications that you follow on [topic of problem]?
* I am working on a product to [solve this problem], can you think of any [features/offerings] you think I should add to my [product/service]?

You want to have less than 10 questions, and keep them open-ended, so that people have a chance to express how they feel about your future product. The goal with these questions is to be brief enough that people don't get annoyed answering them, while giving you the most amount of information you can use to build your product, and give you an idea of how it should be sold and marketed. The pain points they express will not only help you build a better product, but will also give you the exact language to use in your ads and sales pitches. You can also run a similar process once you have your prototype ready. Let a group of your ideal customers use it, play with it, try it on, and give you feedback on what is working well and what needs to be improved.

Once you have your set of questions ready, the next step is to start surveying your future clients. Again, assuming you have no leads and no past clients to call on, you are going to have to get creative with how you reach out to people. However, I think you will be surprised at how much people are willing to help, especially when they know you are trying to build something that might benefit them.

First, start by reaching out to the people in your life. Ask friends, family, friends of friends, and colleagues if they would be willing to chat with you or give you the contact of someone who might. You are looking for people who know you, and wouldn't be afraid of giving you open and honest feedback. Once you exhausted that option, or if you don't have enough people in your network who are a good fit, you'll want to start thinking about where your future clients might hang out. Though you can certainly think of real life places, I am mainly referring to online hangouts. Your ideal client might hang out at Facebook groups, Instagram stories, Pinterest, a specific Subreddit on Reddit, YouTube, or whatever the latest social media outlet is popular at the time you are reading this book. A lot of times, you yourself will already be part of that community so you should have some experience in the etiquette of that space. If not, you will want to join and spend some time learning the best practices. You wouldn't want someone to come to your party and start interrogating people, so take the time to walk around, work the room, get to know people and how they interact, and then you can ask people if they would be interested in having a quick chat or answering a few questions.

When I first started, I did have some people in my network that I reached out to right away, but I also spent some time following moms on Instagram, commenting on their pictures, letting them know I appreciated their content (be careful, people can spot a phony from a mile away, so if you decide to go down this route, be genuine, truthful and really try to get to know the people you are talking to) and once they knew what I was about and that I wasn't trying to shove some product down their throats, then I would message them asking if they would be open for a quick real-life chat with me. These chats eventually led to the format that I still use as the application process for my incubator, and some of the original pain points I heard in these initial interviews can be seen verbatim in my marketing to this day.

Option #2: Ads + Landing Page

If the thought or reaching out to your friends makes you feel uneasy — we'll talk about this later — and hanging out online getting to know people virtually is not your jam, you second option can be to use a combination of a simple ad plus a landing page to gauge people's interest and let them shape your future product. This option does require a bit of money and more technical know how, but it is still just as effective, and since you will most likely have to start placing ads online eventually, it won't hurt to educate yourself a bit on it now.

There so many channels you can use to post an ad online, but I recommend starting with one of the social media platforms. Facebook (which includes Instagram), LinkedIn, Snapchat, Twitter, Reddit, Pinterst and TikTok, for example, all offer marketing platforms that allow you to post ads to audiences customized by you. Again, you will need to at least have an idea of where your ideal future customers hangout, so you can decide which channel is a good place for you to reach them at first. I by no means endorse any platform over another, but for the sake keeping things simple, I will use Facebook's ads manager as a guide here because it is one of the most popular because it has so much reach, and because it's what I mostly use.

Though most channels try to make posting an ad as simple as possible, to start, I recommend you put some time on your handy dandy schedule to just play around the platform. Watch a couple of YouTube videos on the basics (WARNING: do not allow yourself to go into a vortex, please. You want to watch 3 or 4 videos that walk you through the platform and the basics of posting an ad just so you are not completely lost. You really don't need a whole bunch of strategy just yet, and if you get stuck in the complexities of online ads right now, you will lose sight of what matters). Once you feel confident that you can post an ad, you will create a set of ten or so very simple images to use as ads that state the pain points you will be solving. If you haven't interviewed anyone, you will have to guess here, so the first part of your test is to see what pain point actually piques the interest of your desired audience. Here you will be testing to see if people have an urgency to solve the problem in the way you envision. For example, when I was testing out my incubator concept, I created simple ads with statements like the ones below and put them in front of an audience of women who might be interested in starting a business:

- "It's hard to start a business as a busy mom"
- "It's hard to get accepted into incubators"
- "I often get in my own way when trying to start a business"
- "My lack of knowledge stops me from starting a business"

See what I did there? I first wanted to understand if the problems I wanted to solve were things that the people I wanted to reach, actually responded to. And the way I gauged this was by looking at how many clicks each ad got over a very short period of time. If people didn't respond to a certain statement, I right away knew that particular thing was not something I should be worried about solving.

Tech tip: it does not take a lot of money, time, or design skills to run this test. At this point your only focus is on information, not perfection. Do not worry about what your ad looks like, you just want it to be legible and bold enough to make someone to stop scrolling long enough to read it. A good way to accomplish this is by creating an image with two contrasting colors and simple text. This strategy works because we are so used to seeing photos, that when we see two big blocks of colors, it interrupts the pattern in our feed.

Similarly, do not invest a lot of money or time on this test. I started with five dollars per day, and as soon as an ad got to 400 impressions, I would turn it off and read the results. What ever ads got more clicks for less money, I would consider the "winners" (this strategy comes from Mint CRO. They were my coaches when I was starting to lose it with Facebook ads, and showed me some incredible ways to market online). Also, you will need a website link to send people to when you post an ad. Do not stress about this if you don't have one yet. Though you will have to buy a domain name, any domain provider will have the option to let you link your new domain to a "coming soon" page (and that is plenty for now).

After this first part of your test, you will have a set of statements to which people have responded well. The next step is to get people to help you go a little deeper in shaping your product by sending them to a web page that will give more information about your future product and ask them to take some kind of action (in most cases, you will be asking them to give you an email so that you can send them more information once your product is ready). This is called a landing page and again, here you will have dozens of options of providers, so pick the one that you like best and allows you A/B test (meaning it allows you to test multiple versions of the same page at once so you can test what people best respond to, just like what you did with your ads). Most of them will have a drag and drop design platform, which again, you can easily find a couple of video tutorials to help you get started with a basic page design (I have to say it again. Resist the urge to let design take up too much time). The focus of these test landing pages is to let people "vote"' on the features they would like to see in your product, by gauging how they respond to the copy, meaning what you write, on each landing page. You want the copy on your landing page to reference the problem, or problems, you are hoping to solve one more time, so you can then talk about the benefits your product will offer in simple, easy-to-understand language. Once you have that down, the most important part of your landing page will be your call-to-action, meaning the thing you want someone to do on your page that lets you know that what they've read so far sounds like something they are so interested in, they are willing to give you their email, schedule call, or sign up in exchange for what you have to offer. The idea here is to create a few variations of the same page that you can test against one another, and use the winning page to inform you of what people want to see in your product.

I am so happy to be where I am today, but there is a part of me that wishes I could go back in time and show my younger self these steps before spending thousands of dollars and precious hours building something I had not idea people would want. You see, by going out and talking to people about your idea, or spending less than fifty bucks on a simple test, you are guaranteeing that there is an audience for what you want to offer, and building a list of possible clients before you even have anything to sell. Amazing.

What I am sharing with you here is a highly simplified version of what we offer in the incubator, because each business's testing needs are going to be very specific. However, just remember your goal: let your ideal client build your product for you by guiding them with prompts via your ads and landing pages.

Mental Breakdown: Fear of Exposure

One of the things that brings me most joy is seeing women go through this process of validating their ideas in the incubator. A lot of times they come in with just a sliver of an idea, and by the time they are done proving their concept, they know exactly what their business will do. Other times, they are dead set on even the minor details, only to find that they have to make adjustments or even change their original idea entirely based on the feedback from their future customers. It's thrilling to see these women go from the desire for entrepreneurship to stepping into the CEOs they are meat to be.

When you are just starting out, the Proof of Concept is often the first step you take in putting your idea, and therefore, you, "out there". And part of the process does involve reaching out to the people in your life, telling them you are starting something new, asking for help, posting on social media or putting up a simple, not professionally designed website out there for others to see. For someone who is still unsure they can actually do everything they dream of doing, this process can be incredibly intimidating, and the number one thing that comes up for founders at this point is fear of exposure. We are afraid to expose our selves as people who want to do something bold for fear of being mocked either for trying or for failing. We are afraid that someone will steal our idea. We are afraid that people will think we are frauds or not worthy. We are afraid that our lack of experience will show. We let the fear of not knowing what people will think stop us from so many things already, but when it comes to business this fear will not only stop you from creating something amazing, it will rob you of your first customers, and cost you thousands, if not millions of dollars.

To this day, I hesitate before every email I send to my audience, every post I share, and every new video I add to my modules. My first thought is always, "do I actually know what I'm talking about, and who am I to help people start their businesses?" Often a simple post updating the status of my life or my business can spiral into feelings of unworthiness that get me thinking that I don't actually have the expertise to show people what to do because I have failed more times than I can count, I have lost so much money, both mine and other people's, following my passion, and in the process I have hurt myself, and others close to me. I think, if I post about this great thing I did, people will see right through me. They will see that what I do isn't good enough or it isn't innovative enough. They will be reminded of my failures and my faults, and all the legitimacy I've built and all the great work I've done will be a waste. And just when these thoughts start to get the best of me, I remind myself that these feelings are normal. I remember that without my past failures I would never have gotten the inspiration to do what I do. Without having experienced my low points, I wouldn't be able to relate to the women I work with and help them through theirs. These failures, these fears, these low-points, are exactly the things that make my work worth doing. I go back to the testimonials and emails I get from the women I work with, and I am so proud of what they have accomplished. I remind myself that my voice is needed. I tell my self I am worthy of every thing I have because I have created it all myself. And even if all this is not enough to stop me from still getting that pang of fear of exposure, it's enough to get me to send that email or post that picture because on the other side of that fear is another woman who can use my help, and hopefully be inspired to reach out because of something I shared.

Back in Chapter 1, I mentioned that failure is an action, not who you are, so to take a step further, before validating your idea, take some time to get really excited about failing publicly. The proof of concept module in the incubator, is the one module that brings out the most resistance in our founders. I have heard every possible excuse as to why people can't or do not need to go through this step and should skip ahead. But you cannot have a business without customers, and there is no way you will have a successful business if you don't have a dialogue with the people you wish to serve. So if you get hit with a pang of fear just as you are about to send a mass email to your contacts asking if they know anyone who might help you with your survey, remember, exposing yourself or putting yourself out there is imperative to your success as an entrepreneur, so you have to make the choice of whether you would rather stay right where you are or make the jump to something better. If you choose to make the jump, and I hope you do, this is when you will be transformed into a true entrepreneur. Someone who finds joy in creating something of your own, dreaming big, and doing something about it regardless of what others might think.

PERMISSION SLIP:

SHARE YOUR STORY (YOUR VOICE IS NEEDED)

Chapter 6

Partner Up

There are two types of founders I most often encounter in the incubator. One is the person who has always taken care of everything and wants to continue to do it all solo. The other is the person who can't imagine starting something on their own, because they think they are missing something — experience, time, money, confidence, or leadership skills. Both can easily morph into a fear of failure and reluctance to partner up. The reality is that partnership is crucial in entrepreneurship, not because you are not enough, but because learning to collaborate, delegate, compromise, ideate, and give and receive feedback are skills that are used on a daily basis in any successful venture, and the sooner you develop those skills, the better equipped you will be to grow your business.

When 2 Become 1

I admit that even when I was starting the incubator, I struggled with the idea of finding a partner. I had just come off a business failure that had soured a long-term friendship, and I was terrified of disappointing someone like that again. At the time my "I'm not good enough" gremlin was taking over my thoughts pretty consistently, and part of the reason I wanted to go into business again was to avoid falling into depression. I thought that if I could find success in my new business, *then* I would bring in a partner to help me grow. I thought this approach would protect myself and my future partner from disappointment and failure. Obviously the only thing I was doing was giving in to fear and just making things harder on myself, because doing things without support is always harder. Gradually, however, I was able to silence my gremlin, get back to myself, and do the work that always needs to be done after a failure: take stock of my learnings. Once I started that process I quickly realized that if I wanted this to turn into what I envisioned, there was no way I was going to do it alone. I was also able to dissect what hadn't worked previously so I had a good idea of what to try next.

If time is a scarce resource, a partnership is ideal. After you've defined the roles, expectations, and what needs to get done and when, two or three partners with only a few hours per week available are able to accomplish a whole lot more than a single person. And dealing with the administrative part of starting a business — setting up a corporation, registering a name, taking care of accounting, and all that fun stuff — is so much better with a partner. This is classic divide and conquer strategy. This experience will teach you and your partners many of the leadership skills that are crucial for managing a successful business.

One of the things new leaders tend to struggle with is the concept and practice of delegation. Sitting down with your partner to draft a master to-do list, and then figuring out who will take on what role and why, will strengthen your bond, teach you about compromise, and bring to the surface the teamwork challenges you will have to overcome. Most importantly, how founders work with each other will become the foundation for the culture of your organization, so a lot depends on this relationship.

One of the more significant pluses of adding a partner to your startup is expanding your skill pool. So if you haven't done it yet, it's time now to evaluate your skills and what you bring to the table. It's helpful to actually set some time aside, create a document, and basically interview yourself for the job of CEO of your future company. Ask yourself why you want to start this business in the first place and what it is about this business that sparks passion within you. Write down all the reasons you think it's important that you start this business now. What expertise do you have in this area or industry you will be serving? Note the specific skills you possess that make you a good fit for the job. Ask yourself things like: How much money do you actually need to start this business? How much time and money are you willing to invest? How will you recover if it fails? What's the ideal timeline for recovering any expenses and becoming profitable? What is your long-term vision both for yourself and the company?

This is a time for you to be completely honest with yourself about your intentions, your capabilities, and your present situation. The goal is not to discourage you from moving forward, but gain clarity on what kind of partner you should be looking for by establishing the areas where you need help. When looking for a partner you want to find the ying to your yang, not a best friend. When the time comes, you will interview potential partners in the same way you interviewed yourself, because you want to make sure that whoever you bring on has the same level of passion for the idea and the business, and can also contribute skills and time that you don't have.

Of course, you are not *just* looking for skills, you are also looking for a connection, someone with whom you can give and receive honest feedback. The worst thing you can do in the beginning of your partner relationship is create a dynamic where either of you is afraid, or unwilling, to speak the truth. Again, what you are forming here is the beginning of a culture, so this relationship will set the tone for all other relationships in your organization.

My partnership in my manufacturing business went sour right from the start, because I skipped the process of self-interviewing and partnered up without being fully aware of where I needed help. As a result, we were short on some skills and time. Instead of bringing in an additional partner to support these areas, I overcompensated by trying to learn *everything* as I was doing it. Add to that the fact that my partner and I had been friends first, with an already established dynamic, and the inadequacy that I already felt around this person due to my own baggage, and we had a recipe for major conflict and failure.

This isn't to say that you should shy away from partnering with a friend — I know people who have found great success this way. But it is a warning that during this process of self-evaluation and evaluating possible partners, you have to put honesty first. If I had given myself the time to acknowledge that I already felt less accomplished, intelligent, and privileged than my partner, and therefore somewhat guarded around them, I probably could have saved us both a lot of time, money, and ultimately, our friendship by suggesting we bring in a third co-founder.

Another very important aspect you want to be aware of when looking for a partner is their energy. By that I mean, what is their vibe? In conflict, are they the kind of person who often feels like a victim, or are they more likely to get angry and blame others? When everything is going well, do they look for ways to benefit themselves, benefit others, or do they look for win-win situations? Are they good at spotting opportunities in failure? How and when do they celebrate wins? Although it's hard to gauge all this from an interview, you want to get a feel for their nature because along with your energy, this person will also be adding theirs to the DNA of your business. Make sure that even if you don't have much in common, at least you are on the same wavelength, and can get on a path to building something awesome. Lastly, this is someone who you will be spending a lot of time with, and if you can't stand who they are at their core, what's the point?

Wherefore Art Thou, Partner?

If I've successfully convinced you that whatever your business idea, having a partner will help it grow and help build needed leadership skills, you might now be wondering how you can find a co-founder who will be equally passionate about your idea. The simple answer is good old-fashioned networking.

If you have the time and stamina to network in person, then start by searching event websites for get-togethers happening around you. Commit to attending a minimum number of events per month. When I was first starting out in Leadership Development coaching, I really wanted to help women in tech, so I scoured websites like Eventbrite and MeetUp for any event that might draw these women. No matter how tired or grumpy I was, I made myself attend at least 2 events per week. That led me to meeting the incredible people behind organizations like Tech Ladies, SHeo, Amy's Smart Girls, and Quilt. These events brought me my first paying clients, but perhaps more importantly, I was there to let these organizations know that I had something to offer, and was open to helping. So I kept in touch with the organizers and eventually this led to speaking gigs at General Assembly, Women's Empower X, and Tech Ladies.   T h e s e events led me to Ladies Get Paid, where I met one of my partners in DEI work, Kellie Wagner, the founder of Collective - a DEI Lab. One thing I love about my journey to finding Kellie is that, though I heard about Ladies Get Paid from someone I met in a real life event, I "met" Kellie via chat on a Slack channel, which led to a phone conversation, but it wasn't until we had already been working together for almost a year that I actually met her in person.

This roundabout journey is what I love most about networking. If you show up with the spirit of genuinely wanting to be of service and keep in touch with the people you connect with, the possibilities are endless for who you will meet and what bonds you will form. Even today, I work with and partner with women on a daily basis who I have never actually met in person, so don't think that you need to be tied to any geographical area when you start your search. For all you know, your soulmate business partner may live on the other side of the world.

Unbounded accessibility is one of the biggest perks of networking in the twenty-first century. If time is tight, you can't get a babysitter, or you simply prefer it, you can network without leaving your home. This work is very similar to what you've already accomplished finding the ideal audience for your proof of concept. Now you need to figure out where your future partner might be hanging out online, and go find her. My personal preference is to make the rounds, get to know people, offer help, and feel out the vibe in the virtual room to gauge how receptive people are before an ask. But I have seen lots of people have success walking into an online group and straight up announce that they are looking for a partner or co-founder with a particular set of skills to help launch a business. Either tactic can work, so go with what feels most natural to you.

The Vetting Process

Once you find someone who has an interest, or even if you already know someone interested in going into business with you, the easiest way to make sure you will both be on the same page is to use the self-evaluation model from earlier in the chapter as your interview guide. You want to come prepared to fill her in on your complete vision for both the day-to-day operations and the future of your venture. Awareness of your values, the kind of company you want to build, the timeline you have in mind, the amount of involvement and input you will commit to, your short and long-term vision, and what you expect from her will enable your potential partner to more accurately reflect on the partnership you are proposing and give you an honest answer about whether she thinks it's a good fit.

You want to find someone who both fills the gaps and is super stoked to join you. When you find that kick-ass person who ticks all the boxes, do a favor to both of you and your business, and make things official.

Partner Contracts

I'll keep this brief. There is no reason to put yourself through the misery of having to figure out what happens if you and your partner get into a disagreement. Once you find the ideal person with whom you'll build your dream business, sign a contract. Get that shit on paper ahead of time, and don't get greedy or start thinking too far into the future. If you and your partner can't agree on what's fair in a partner contract before the business is making any money, then it's not a good partnership. If that's the case, take your idea, move on, and look for another partner. Many people fail in their partnerships before they even begin, but there are plenty of great people out there.

Accountability Partner

If after reading all of this you are still not convinced that a partner is right for you at this moment, I strongly suggest you go for the next best option — an accountability partner (AP). For the same reasons that you are more likely to exercise if you have a personal trainer, having an accountability partner will give you all the benefits you get from a corporate environment without the commitment of having a co-founder. The great thing about this kind of partnership is that anyone who has the same availability as you do can be a good partner. So if you have a friend who is also starting a business, or a mom friend who works from home, this kind of arrangement is easy to set up and mutually beneficial.

An accountability partner is someone with whom you can either work with or check in with on a consistent basis to keep you on track so you follow through on your goals. Once I discovered how much more productive I was when I started working with my accountability partner, I wondered how I had ever gotten anything done before her. Remember I talked about the trap of staying busy, but not accomplishing anything? An accountability partner not only keeps you on track, but helps you work smarter with the time you have.

There are many ways to work with a partner in this way, but the strategy that works best for me and the women in the incubator is to treat your partner as a colleague or co-worker. The way I structure my work with my AP is first, we get together and go over our schedules to see what times we both have available, then create a cadence in both our calendars, or appointments for those times which includes a link to meet up virtually. (As you can tell by now, I am a huge fan of anything I can do from home, mostly because I don't want commute times chiseling away at the time I do have available). Some people prefer to meet face-to-face, however, at a library or a co-working space.

Once we have the next 3 or 4 months mapped out, we stick to those appointments. No matter what is happening, we commit to treating our time just as we would a real job. Like a regular day job, once we are both "in the room," we don't have to chit chat or keep constant tabs on one another, we simply get to work. If you haven't worked in this way before, it may seem a little weird for two people to be on a video meeting not actually chatting, but you will quickly find that just having someone there with you who is also committed to being productive will change how you work. More than that, this journey can be so lonely at times that you run the risk of quitting before you've given yourself a chance to succeed, just because it's tough to go at it alone. So having someone who knows your goals, has your back, and can be there to call you out when you are falling behind might make the difference between you launching or not.

Business Coach

When it comes to accountability, adding to skills or knowledge you may be missing, or getting over any mental or emotional hurdles, by far the most fruitful investment you can make will be a business coach. Yes, I am biased, but the reason I became one is because I remember starting something on my own and having no idea that a coach was even an option.

There aren't a lot of entrepreneurs in my family, I didn't go to business school, and I didn't have any mentors who had their own businesses. Growing up, I was surrounded by women who put in a lot of sweat taking care of shit on their own. But the lack of representation in my life, and lack of experience seeing successful people seek others for help when needed trained me to think that the only way to get anything done was to suck it up and figure it out. I knew how to be resourceful and resilient, sure, but often did twice the work necessary because every time

I needed something it was like reinventing the wheel. The thought of asking for help rarely entered my mind.

Smart people invest in access to people who know more than they do, and even big time CEOs still use business coaches. Regardless of whether you have a co-founder, or an amazing accountability partner, you absolutely should invest in a coach. I don't usually allow myself to dive into what-ifs or should-haves, but when I do I always kick myself for not getting a business coach for my boutique or my manufacturing business. The only way to overcome not knowing what we don't know, and setting ourselves up for a win is to surround ourselves with people who are ten steps ahead of where we want to be.

Mental Breakdown: I Can Do This Alone

If you've also lacked the privilege of learning from successful people growing up, or had to build yourself up in life, it's completely understandable that you might choose to skip the partnership step.

I remember rationalizing that if I kept my insecurities and doubts to myself, or tried to figure things out by myself, I could avoid experiencing the embarrassment of seeing other's disappointment if I failed. But every single time I kept quiet when things became too much for me to handle, or was afraid to admit that I didn't know what I was doing and seek help, problems would end up getting bigger and spilling over. This would leave me completely defeated, validating yet again my feelings of not being good enough. Eventually this turned into a cycle that manifested itself in all areas of my life. I would start something, get overwhelmed, not ask for help, make my problems bigger, and this bubble of problems would burst, thereby ensuring that I, and anyone who was near me at the time, would suffer in the fallout.

No matter how much I emphasize the benefits, or how easy I make it, many people in the incubator opt out of finding a co-founder or an accountability partner. You won't be the first person to disregard this advice if you decide to do the same. The difference is that my founders have a coach as well as mentors, however, so I give them a pass — for a little while. But for you, wherever you are and no matter why you think you can't reach out to others, I am here for you. My personal email is at the end of this book and even if it takes me a while, I will answer. The first step is on you, though, so reach out and ask for help. After that, you will need a plan.

PERMISSION SLIP:

WHEN YOU NEED HELP, ASK

Chapter 7

Make It Official

Back when I was planning the launch of my boutique, before Instagram and the ubiquity of the "overnight entrepreneur", most people still believed in the business plan and followed the age-old rules and bureaucracy of starting a business as it has been done traditionally. I remember spending hours working on my business plan, creating projections for the next five years, filing trademarks and copyrights, and wondering what it was all for. While I do believe in planning and setting goals, after countless goal-setting sessions and endless planning, I find that what works best for me is the outline+basics strategy. This strategy allows you to have a plan and prepare for the road ahead without getting tripped up by details and perfection.

Business Guide

I'll go ahead and say it: You don't need a business plan right now. What you do need is to know what problem your company will solve, who needs this problem solved, why they need you to solve this problem, and what solution you will use to solve it. You will also need to know how much it will cost to run this business, where you will find the people who will buy from you, how your business will make money, and how you will measure your success. That's pretty much it.

You don't need a plan when you are starting out, you need a guide. A plan can restrict you, while a guide leaves room for you to adapt, shift, and pivot when needed. If you stick to focusing on the things I listed above, when you hit a snag or fail to see growth, you can easily reference your guide and determine where you need to focus to overcome your present challenge.

Let's say you're selling a physical product, and you know exactly where your customers are, you're doing a great job reaching them, they are buying, the reviews are great, you know your solution is working, yet the profit is still not there. In this scenario, you can look at your guide, tick the boxes that are working, and then set to work on what needs improvement. (In this case, either the cost of doing business or your measurements of success.)

One of my favorite tools for creating an easy guide is the Lean Business Canvas™. If you are already familiar with the Lean Startup™ methodology, you probably have seen this. If not, a quick Google search can help you find a PDF version. Essentially it is a one-page business plan that shows you how to define the essentials you need to keep in mind for your business. Again, the idea is to keep you focused on what's important for your business day-to-day and get you away from spending too much time on bogus predictions.

Make It Legal

I may not be a big fan of business plans, but when it comes to making sure you protect yourself and your future business, I strongly recommend you make things legal as soon as you can. The last thing you want to worry about is paying back taxes or having your business shut down because you failed to file the right paperwork. Obviously, I won't offer any specific advice here because laws and requirements vary so much between countries, states, and counties. Keeping with the theme from

Chapter 6, I encourage you to ask for help with this step, even if you think you've done enough research. Most local governments have resources to help entrepreneurs understand the steps required to operate a business — but when in doubt, outsource. By formalizing your business early on, you are making a commitment to see it all the way through to operation, while taking steps to protect yourself from future headaches.

For me, this is the kind of work that can easily delay or interfere with actually doing business. Rather than wasting an hour on Google trying to figure things out on your own, spend that time finding an expert and getting a quote for what it will cost to have them do it. If you have money to invest, this is an area I highly recommend you do. This advice also applies to accounting. Hold off while you can, but as soon as you start investing money into your business or start making money from it, it's time to hire a professional. This is an area where a good financial coach would also be money well-spent if you have the resources.

Business Structures, Taxes, Morals, and Ethics

When you start down the path of legalizing your business, you will be faced with decisions about what business structure works best for long-term protection and what kind of taxes you will be responsible for. One thing to note here is that, at least in the US, you have options to incorporate your businesses in different states and because each state has their own set of regulations and protections for businesses, people often choose to incorporate in states that are more "business friendly." So it will be of great benefit to you and the reputation of your company to revisit your personal and business values before making decisions.

We often think of taxes as a burden we want to escape from, and forget how we benefit from them on a daily basis. If you pause to think about it, where you decide to pay your business taxes matters more than simply saving a few bucks at the end of the fiscal year. I challenge you to think about your community and why it matters — or not — that your business be a contributor to those who live and work where you operate. The important thing here is that you make these choices consciously, by checking them against your values. For me, when I was registering my LLC, I had the option to incorporate in Delaware, a state known for offering more incentives to businesses. But I value being a social enterprise, and opting for Delaware instead of California, where I was actually going to be conducting business, felt like a hypocritical move that went against the ethos of my mission. So in that case, I chose to register my business in California, even though it meant I would have to take a bigger hit when tax season rolled around.

I deliberately kept this chapter short and sweet because this is the least sexy aspect of launching a business. The task of making things official and legal may be tedious, but none of these things are worth getting tripped up over. Start your business, do the best you can, and move ahead even if you can't figure everything out right now. Hire a professional as soon as you can later on down the line.

Mental Breakdown: Why Bother?

I still, to this day, delay the legalizing process as long as I possibly can. I already do so much administrative work at home that just the thought of adding these kinds of tasks to the list of things I have to organize and manage makes me want to lie down and take a nap. When I started, however, this resistance came from an entirely different place. My thinking then was, "I'm not even really doing any business yet, and I don't even know if this will turn into anything, so why bother now?" Can you see what's wrong with this kind of thinking? If you don't have enough confidence in what you are doing to think it will become a full-blown business, it won't.

Thinking you can delay this process until you make enough sales, have "x" number of clients, or any other excuse only shows your lack of commitment and belief in yourself. Going through this process now will have the opposite effect. Imagine getting the approval for your official business name, finding out that your trademark application was approved, or opening a bank account specifically for your business. These kinds of things are a confidence booster, and feel like a permission slip to do great things. Going through this process is worth it, if only for the feeling that from this point on, nothing stands in the way of you doing great things.

PERMISSION SLIP:

WHEN IN DOUBT, OUTSOURCE

Chapter 8

Money Mindset

Okay, here we go. Before you start this chapter, I advise you to get comfy, grab your yummy drink of choice, and take a couple of deep breaths.

So much of running a business is about money. Most business's success is measured by how much money they make, and money is a huge motivator. No matter your role, you have to be mindful of how you are spending, earning, or saving money for the company.

We all deal with money on a daily basis, yet I have never met a person who doesn't have a complicated relationship with it, whether they recognize it or not. Regardless of your background and how satisfied or dissatisfied you may be at the moment with your money situation, before you move forward in your entrepreneurial journey you must confront and repair your relationship with money. I don't want you to go into this thinking this is going to be hard or unpleasant, however. The great thing about this process is that it has the potential to improve SO many areas of your life. My hope is that once you get started you will have the foundation and motivation to keep doing this on your own. This is much bigger than a single chapter in a book.

Money Story

The best place to start is always at the beginning. Allowing yourself to reflect on your money story will give you clues for where to focus your attention when doing this work. Even after big business fails, I didn't think to look into my own money story. I stood looking at statements and a decline in income, and never noticed the connection between how I was thinking about and treating money and my business stumbles. I remember clearly thinking that *I* was a failure, and mentally listing all the ways I hadn't been smart enough or good enough, or the right person to do the job. I never thought specifically about how my relationship with money had also played a role in those businesses not working. Luckily, the business coach I hired to assist me in my third launch encouraged me to explore this relationship. Gradually, that guilt and those feelings of failure gave way to a new awareness and an eagerness to learn from my past and approach the topic of money from a completely new angle. The first time I sat down to write and confront my money story, it became immediately obvious I wasn't going to grow anything until I got a lot more intimate with money, and a lot less scared to face it head on.

My money story goes something like this: For a long time I was a single child of a single mother who worked a full-time job. I remember hearing the words "We can't afford it" on occasion, but generally I never wanted for much. We always had a comfortable place to live, I was able to go to dance lessons, swim class, after school English classes, summer camps, vacations. What I don't remember are conversations about money. We never talked about where it came from, where it went, what was important, or what I should think about when I eventually had any of my own. I honestly cannot recall a single time when I was taught any lesson about money.

When I moved to the United States at thirteen, I was introduced to the novel concept of baby-sitting, and this was the first way I earned money on my own. This being my first time earning money, I would have benefitted from a lesson or two, but I don't remember anyone sitting me down to explain the basics of accounting, savings, or investing.

When I turned seventeen I had the incredible opportunity to study abroad for a few months. This is when I got my first bit of financial direction in the form of a credit card and the words "use it only in case of an emergency," which to my seventeen year-old self meant food, clothes, and fun. I vaguely remember being reprimanded about my spending, but don't recall any real consequences. By the time I got to college, I was immediately signed up for a credit card by a very nice young person outside a campus building. That card was promptly maxed out, and again I remember just a generic warning from my mother, but no real direction.

Though we never had any real sit-downs about money, the silence around it and failure to confront it directly taught me lessons that shaped my relationship with money for years. My mother did the best she could, and I still hope to make it up to her for all I put her through, especially financially, but because she wasn't aware that money could and should have been talked about frequently, I learned that I should just deal with it on my own, no matter how much help I needed. And because my mother was willing to bail me out so many times, I also ended up internalizing that somehow, money was always available, no matter how much I screwed up. We both would have benefited from having open and honest conversations about our financial situation and how money should be handled.

My public education also fell short by not teaching basic financial literacy to young people. And my experience with abuse helped me view my money mishaps as personal flaws for which I had to feel shame and guilt. So with this lovely combination of lessons, I was molded into a person with little self-control when it came to money, who had no idea how to manage the money I did have, and who felt a deep shame that prevented me from asking for help when I needed it. Basically, I was the embodiment of the worst kind of person to start a business.

The beauty of facing your own money story is that rather than making it about blame or shame, you get to see clearly how your relationship with money was formed, and the lessons you internalized, so you can finally move beyond them. If you grew up hearing that you didn't have enough, you might have formed the idea that there is never enough money, and that it's a struggle to get it. On the other hand, If you grew up with a lot of money, you might correlate earning money with a pressure to succeed. It's only when you see the stories you've been telling yourself clearly that you can start to write new ones.

For me that rewriting happened when I reached for the tools that I needed. I found a financial coach who empathetically guided me out of my shame, I read books, and I did a lot self-soothing. The one thing I knew was that I was neither happy staying where I was, nor willing to continue going down the same path. Ultimately, I was able to reframe my story, and see the benefits that worked for me.

For example, the sense that money somehow is always available is something I still rely on, and often use as a mantra. I very frequently will look at my partner and express my amazement at how we always have the money we need to live the life we want. We have come to believe this deeply, and express gratitude for the truth in it often. Maybe for you, having been taught the lesson that money is made to be saved has made you anxious about spending. But if you choose to reframe it and own the fact that you are good at saving money, you can turn that anxiety into a knowing that no matter how much you spend, you are still good at saving.

I know I am not alone when it comes to feelings of shame around money, so whatever your story, facing this shame is inevitable to overcoming it. Bari Tesler, in The Art of Money, shares that shame thrives in secrecy, so the easiest way out of shame is to talk about it. I know this is easier said than done, but try taking baby steps and see how you feel. Call a good friend and share with her that you've been feeling overwhelmed by your debt, or send a text to your sister about how embarrassed you are about being the only one in the family who doesn't have her money situation together yet. Ask for help. The sooner you can start owning your money story, the sooner you can take the next step toward having a healthier money mindset.

Making Peace With Your Money Present

The first and most critical step in rewriting your money story is to make peace with wherever that story has led you. For many people, this process feels like a big stretch, and I get how hard it can be to decide to be happy and grateful for whatever you have going on financially, especially since we are so used to bitching and moaning about it. All. The. Time.

I used to be a freaking pro at neglecting my bank account and credit card statements. I could go weeks without looking at them, which made whipping out my card to pay for things a mini roller coaster ride. For those of you who get me, I'm talking about that feeling in your stomach, the slight panic attack you experience every time you hand your card to someone, wondering if the transaction will go through. It took me a while, but once I started to do this work I realized that was no way to live. I finally saw it for what it was — that damn feeling of shame showing up again, in yet another area of my life.

To help shift my mindset so that I could start to face my present money reality, I started to think about money as a best friend. I started to ask myself how I could be a better friend to money and how I expected money to treat me. I made a promise to be more present for my money, and to check in on it more often. Even a quick glance at my current statement can, like a quick text, let a friend know that you are thinking of them. Then every few weeks, I could have a more lengthy hear-to-heart with my money, where I would sit down, budget, and plan.

It's also important to express gratitude for a good friend, so I took time to acknowledge all the times money had been there for me when I needed it, and how it kept showing up for me even when I was talking shit about it behind its back. I promised to put in the work to be kinder, more attentive, and more committed to making this relationship last. I also promised to accept money for what it is, so I checked all my accounts, looked at my balances, and made peace with what was there without criticizing where it was short and where it could lose a few pounds (or dollars).

For a lot of us, especially those of us who love to ignore our problems, this can be a difficult exercise. It helps to remember that whatever your current situation, it is a story of who you have been up to this point, and does not reflect who you are now deciding to be. Also, we're so used to complaining, avoiding the issue, and generally being unhappy at what we see as lack, that it's almost a knee-jerk reaction to look at our balances and think "not enough." So to make things a little easier, find room for fun and joy in this process. For me what that looked like was changing all my account names and passwords to things that would make me smile every time I looked at it: MoneyandIareBFFFs, MoneyHasMyBack, ILoveMoney&MoneyLovesMe. I also made sure that every time I was about to dive deep into my finances that I was in a good, relaxed mood, or I would move that appointment with myself to a different time in my calendar. These are strategies that will help you not only be okay with wherever you may be now, but will serve as a foundation as you start to write new chapters in your money story from this point on.

Speaking Your (New) Truth

By now you have probably heard a version of the following statement in a million ways, but it's worth repeating: your thoughts form your words, which guide your actions, which create your reality. They just do. So before we move on, let me rephrase it so it sinks in: thoughts form words, which guide actions, which create reality. So your thoughts create your reality. Got it?

With that being the undisputed truth, how can you go about creating a new money story, and money reality, for yourself? You think it into existence. Now that you know that you are not going to develop into the badass CEO version of yourself unless you get ahold of your old money story and create yourself a new one, it's time to start thinking like the person who does have it in them to be that badass boss.

The best advice for people who have a desire to develop new habits is, decide what you want to be, then act like it. So when you think about the entrepreneur, CEO, or business owner you want to be, you want to think about money the way *she* thinks about money. And how does this CEO version of yourself think about money? She has a good handle on it, knows how to manage it well, isn't desperate for it, and is secure in thinking that it is always coming her way. She is confident in how she invests it and knows how to get a return for whatever she spends. She believes with the core of her being that she is meant to be leading, meant to be growing her business, and most importantly, that she *deserves* to live the lifestyle she wants and earn whatever she needs to live that lifestyle. The moment you can look in the mirror and see that you are this person, and all you have to do is catch up to that vision, you are ready to rewrite your money story.

One thing about rewriting your money story, however, is that it can be kind of a lonely thing to go through. Unlike other areas of your life where we can more easily seek the opinions of others for encouragement, money tends to carry a different weight, and people feel more entitled to judge you for it. Not only that, we often judge ourselves and keep dreaming small for fear of being judged. It can be easy to let others know that you want to start a business, and a lot of people will most likely encourage you to do so, but the moment you tell them you want to start a business so you can buy one of those cool new electric cars, or so you can send your kid to a private school abroad, or so you can buy a trip to the moon, out comes the side-eyes and scoffs. Fuck that. Let go of thinking that there is a limit to what you deserve. Let go of guilt around what you desire. It's completely normal to want more, and letting shame win yet another round here won't do you or anyone else any good.

Mental Breakdown

Since this whole chapter is one big mental breakdown, I wanted to add something that for me has been incredibly valuable when it comes to dealing with things that I feel insecure about: Gratitude.

Sure, the put together, smart, confident business owner version of you can feel miles away from where you are now, but like every other journey of self-empowerment, gratitude will be your secret weapon. The more you find to be grateful for, and appreciative of, the more your thoughts start to change. You can start small, and be grateful that you are finally giving yourself permission to look at money differently, or be grateful that even though you have a balance on your credit card, it means that money was there for you when you needed it. Take a moment to actually write down all the ways in which you are grateful to be where you are now. It doesn't matter that you don't have, or aren't everything you want at this exact moment. What matters is that you see your current situation for what it is: the space that you will lead to where you want to be.

PERMISSION SLIP:

YOU CAN REWRITE THE MONEY STORY YOU DESERVE

Chapter 9

Good Investments, Money Wasters, and Funding

G rowing up, I always loved the last days of summer because they signaled that it was time to go shopping for new school supplies. Browsing through the aisles of colorful pens and crisp new notebooks gave me a sense of hope and excitement for the new year. I regularly notice this same enthusiasm in founders in the incubator, except that instead of a glittery new pen, they lust after fancy custom websites and advertising campaigns.

You had little control in the early years of your personal money story, but hopefully you've gained some clarity around your relationship with money and are ready to write your money future in a way that serves you. And this newfound clarity means that you also get to create a money story for your business in a way that serves *it*.

Over the years that I have been guiding people, I have seen a pattern emerge in the early days of a business. People tend to waste money in predictable ways, as well as fail to invest in some necessities. I have dubbed these: *The Big 4*, or *Money Wasters vs. Good Investments*. Before you hire that cool designer to build you an amazing website, let's take a closer look at The Big 4.

Money Waster #1: Custom Design

Listen, I totally get it — when things look good, they tend to demand a certain respect. I remember spending *hours* on website design and revisions for the latest logo options from my designer. I figured no one would trust a business with a run-of-the-mill website or random logo. Also, design does fill you with a sense of excitement, the feeling that you are seeing your business finally come to fruition. Luckily, by the time I launched my consulting business, I had finally learned the truth. These things, however "crucial" you think they are, ultimately are not what bring your business to life. A gorgeous website does not make you money. A great product, the right messaging, good reviews, and knowing where to reach your customers... these are the things that make a business successful.

I have seen clients so resistant to moving forward until the perfect branding is in place, that a year after they started working on their business they still have nothing to show for it. All because they don't have the "right" look yet — how crazy is that!? Imagine you hire someone to manage a boutique for you, and a year later they hadn't even opened the doors because they hadn't found the right clothes to put on the mannequin in the window. You would surely fire them.

Design is important, and having a cohesive brand look does give your business a certain air of professionalism, but if it's keeping you from moving forward in your business — or worse — taking up a huge chunk of your budget, let it go. At least for now anyway. Once you are rolling in cash, go ahead, spend hours pouring over logo concepts, and brand colors. But until then, focus on finding clients who are desperate for what you have so you can start to build your reputation and optimize your sales funnel.

Caveat: If you have a design-based business, and your bread and butter depends on design (be honest about this), then by all means design your little heart out, as long as it isn't costing you too much money, not taking up too much time, or keeping you from bringing in and serving new clients.

Smart Investment #1: Technology

The beauty of modern technology is that even if you can't bring yourself to move forward before everything looks "perfect," there are many tools at your disposal to help you create something beautiful without wasting a lot of time or money. With the help of a website builder and hosting software, you can have a gorgeous website that serves the basic functions you need, up and running in less than day.

Investing in the right kind of tech tools can help you move your business forward in so many ways. For example, simple accounting software will serve to keep you on track from the very beginning, even if you cannot yet afford an accountant. Or a scheduling tool can make the process of connecting with your new customers much simpler. A customer management service will keep you organized so you can stay on top of who you've already reached out to and who needs a little more love. Even without having a huge staff, a team management application can completely change your life by helping you and your partner organize, divide, and prioritize your to-do's. Basically, there is a tool out there for anything you can think of, and if it'll help you save time, money, or effort, it's worth looking into.

Technology is also a huge crutch to new founders who do not have the budget for a team, but still need to accomplish a wide variety of tasks. My coaching and consulting businesses for example, could essentially be run by one person, yet I could not operate effectively without the 21 different software service providers we currently use. This may sound like a crazy bananas number of things to keep track of, but each serves a specific function that either saves me time, brings in more clients, or makes my client experience better, and all ultimately save me money.

In my business, I leverage technology for the following the functions:

- Email
- Video Conferencing
- International Calling
- Landing Pages
- Advertising
- Email Marketing Automation
- Visual Insights and Website Data
- Payment Processing

- Project Management
- Course Hosting Platform
- Webinar Hosting
- Graphic Design
- Web Design and Hosting
- Scheduling
- Email Tracking
- Social Proof Tracking
- Accounting
- Social Media Content Management
- Focus Tool

This list may appear overwhelming to you, but each of these represents something that directly links to either customer satisfaction or sales, which for me are the two most important aspects of my day-to-day. So again, I challenge you to examine how you are currently running your business and find places where software could make things easier for you.

Caveat: Make sure you are investing in technology that you actually need right now. Resist the urge to buy into a product that you do not need at the moment. Also, the majority of available tools offer free trials or a free version, so always opt for that first before adding another expense to your monthly budget.

Money Waster #2: Bad Advertising

The moment you put up that website, or create your first social media profile, it's normal to be excited about spreading the word about your product or service. I recommend you spend little to no money on advertising in your early days, however. While creating an ad and putting it on a social media platform is pretty easy, fully understanding the system, and the whys of online advertising, is extremely complex. So unless you are already an expert on advertising and you know you can kick-ass, I strongly encourage you to wait. Getting a return for your investment in advertisement can be extremely difficult, and it takes a lot of testing until you find what works for you. Until you have some cash to throw around, and time to wait to see a return, don't start throwing money into the hands of the big dogs (Google, Facebook, etc.).

I was such a sucker in the beginning. Every time I would get a suggestion to "boost" a post or "promote" a story, I would click that button and next thing I knew 50 bucks had flown out the window with no chance of it ever coming back. I figured, hey, at least I am getting exposure. But who cares about your ad being shown to a bunch of people who may not connect to your message or what you are offering, and will more likely than not just scroll right past it?

Smart Investment #2: Marketing Education or Professionals

The obvious answer to bad advertising is good advertising. When you are starting out, however, it is hard to tell the difference. This is why I highly encourage you to educate yourself on how good marketing and advertising should perform. Coming from the Advertising Technology world, I can tell you that oftentimes even the professionals may not have the answer. Investing in knowledge around this topic allows you to take control and find confidence in an area that mystifies many entrepreneurs, who often end up losing money to "professionals."

You will want to understand the basics of audience analytics, advertising performance, pricing, average conversion rates, rates of return, compelling assets, and enticing copywriting, so that when you decide to start advertising, you don't just throw spaghetti at the wall to see what sticks. Understanding how this stuff works will give you a sense of confidence and control over a very important part of your business.

Once you have this basic understanding, then look into professionals. I do recommend investing in an expert in this field because marketing truly is a full-time job when you are a novice, so unless you have the time, outsourcing should save you time and get you the biggest return for your investment. And once you start looking for someone, you will understand why educating yourself is so important. Armed with knowledge, you can tell your pro exactly what you expect to see in a campaign, how you want it to perform, and what success will look like, without being overwhelmed by unfamiliar terms or unprepared without the necessary data.

Once I realized that I had no idea what I was doing when it came to effective marketing and online advertising, I happily dove into education. I am fortunate to take easily to new technology, and I love to learn about every aspect of my business so when I eventually outsource or hire someone to take over a task, I can more easily understand what I am looking for, and the challenges they will face. When I hired an advertising expert who had the data and TONS of satisfied customers to back up her claims, I joined her mastermind group and dedicated at least an hour, most days more, to learning her strategies. Now instead of following a prompt and randomly boosting a post into an ad, I know how to create an ad that speaks directly to my ideal customers and grabs the attention of people who are most likely to connect with me and my brand. I also know what makes an ad successful, and most importantly, how to determine when something isn't going to bring me a return so I can quickly shut it off and move on to what works.

Money Waster #3: Premises

Unless you dream of having a brick and mortar business or an office that will directly impact your profits, do not spend money on office space, furniture, or nonessential extras. Even if you have extremely ambitious plans for your startup and have plenty of money to burn, there is no need for that money to go towards a fancy space. I already mentioned my affinity for remote first, but even if you see it as crucial that you and your team work out of the same space, there are so many places you can use as your startup headquarters that do not require you to sign a lengthy lease, or buy a lot of office extras. I am a huge fan of libraries, coworking spaces, hotel lobbies, and of course, home offices.

On the other hand, you do want to create a space you can "escape" to that makes you feel like you are "at work." I encourage investing in little things to make that happen, like an office chair for your desk or a space divider to create an office in your living room. You want to have a routine that signals to your brain that this is work time and free yourself from as many distractions as possible. Generally an office does make it easier to create a collaborative work environment for your team, but since you most likely do not have a huge team right now, leave that expense for later.

Smart Investment #3: Accounting, Tax, and Business Professionals

One of the biggest blind spots for new entrepreneurs is determining what investments are paying off and what expenses are redundant, so hiring a professional to keep track of these things for you right from the beginning will save a lot of money in the long run. Sure, an accountant may be a big expense when you haven't made any sales, but you can track your money with software in the beginning, and if you choose an accounting software provider that also offers live help, you actually end up getting the benefits of an accountant without the price tag.

Where you do not want to skimp, however, is when hiring a tax professional. There is no reason you should try to navigate a complex tax system if you don't have to. There are so many ways a tax professional can give you insights into how to leverage the benefits available to new entrepreneurs, and in my opinion taking the time to do the research yourself is just not worth it. Furthermore, the system changes constantly, so information you can use this year might be useless by the next tax season.

A third professional I highly recommend having by your side is a business mentor or coach, as I explained in Chapter 6. There is no substitute to having someone who knows your industry well, can guide you, help you grow, and encourage you in the moments when you start to doubt yourself.

I admit that it took me forever to finally realize that having someone manage my money was a good idea, but one area I never had any doubt about was investing in business coaching. To date, I have invested almost US$30,000 in coaching and I can honestly trace back every dollar I have made since to conversations I had with my coaches.

Money Waster #4: Buying Things That Should Be Built Organically

It is common to look at your newly created social media profiles and wonder how you will ever build an audience quickly enough to have a good reputation. You may find yourself considering a short cut — buying a few followers, hiring a company to follow and comment on people's posts for you, or buying an email list just to get things started. Don't do it.

The point of leveraging social media as a marketing tool is to find and connect with real people who fit the profile of your ideal customer, NOT to have the most followers. And the only way to ensure that the people who do follow you have a chance to become genuine buyers is to create content that connects and prompts them to engage. This is truly an area where it is all about quality and not quantity. Even if it takes a while to build an online community of 100 ardent fans who absolutely love what you do and say, those 100 people are a heck of a lot more valuable than 10,000 people who may never even look at your posts, much less comment or engage with them.

Smart Investment #4: Insurance

It may not be sexy or elicit an exciting response from you, but insurance is SO VERY important and something that many first time entrepreneurs neglect. It is tempting to skip this step because, again, in the beginning you are doing very little business, so it seems unnecessary. But you truly never know what could happen, and if you already have a tight startup budget, you want to avoid unexpected expenses that can be covered by having a good insurance policy in place.

For readers in countries without universal healthcare, I also strongly recommend you get yourself some health insurance. It is safer for you, and for your family. You don't want to have to quit your new business because of an unforeseen medical expense.

Of course there are many other things that people tend to overinvest or underinvest in when it comes to a new business, but from my experience, these are the 4 areas where I see most people stumble. Now I'm the kind of person who loves to invest in things that will make my life easier, but when I look back I can see how many times I threw money at things that didn't bring me anything in return and only served to get me to closer to shutting down by business. You too will wonder if something you are about to invest in is truly worth it. Ask yourself these questions in order to make that determination:

- Will it bring me new clients?
- Will it make it easier for me to find new clients?
- Will it make it faster for me to attract clients?
- Will it help my existing clients stay or return?
- Will it improve my clients' experience?
- Will it improve my product or service in any way?
- Will it make it safer or easier for me to conduct business?

If you cannot immediately answer any of these questions with a resounding "yes!,' with the data to back it up, then you should probably hold off on it.

Mental Breakdown: Lack Mindset

Back when I used to avoid looking at my bank account, every little expense filled me with anxiety. Every spending decision felt like a gamble. Every time I agreed to hire someone new, I would wonder if I would have enough to pay them. Every time I was late on a payment, I felt shame about what that said about me. Now I can see that all those thoughts were coming from the same place: a lack mentality.

Focusing on what you don't have, worrying if you have enough, and doubting you are capable of getting a return for what you spend are surefire ways to keep you exactly where you are. It is so easy to go to a place of lack, simply because it is everywhere. The news is a fountain of information about how we are in shortage of everything and are all doomed, so it's no wonder we bring this in to our day-to-day. This pervasiveness also gives us a false lack mindset and makes us believe in competition — if someone else has more, then we must have less.

Swapping out your lack mindset for one of abundance will ease your anxieties and change your reality. I want more than anything for this to be a joyful and fun journey for you. Believing — and I mean truly believing — that you live and attract abundance requires practice, but it will change your motivation for doing the work you do. To shift your mindset, you need to create a practice of reframing where you see lack, and appreciating the abundance that already surrounds you. Because we are bombarded with news of lack everywhere, creating a specific ritual will make it easier to create that shift within you.

One of my favorite ways of doing that is journaling. I take 5 minutes every day to write down all the ways in which I am surrounded by abundance (love, friends, fresh air, good food, etc). Some people bring this to their meditative practice, while others create mantras. Try it all out, and stick with what feels natural and works for you. It might take a few days or weeks, but the result is waking up every day excited for another day of work because you absolutely love what you are doing, as opposed to feeling desperate to sign another client or make another sale because you feel you don't have enough.

In the next chapter we will look at ways to fund your business, a topic that inherently comes from lack because you may not have enough money to start on your own. But if you approach it from a mindset of knowing there are people out there who are eager to help you get started, even the daunting task of fundraising can be fun.

PERMISSION SLIP:

YOU CAN BE
HAPPY ABOUT
WHERE YOU ARE
NOW (WITHOUT
WORRYING
ABOUT WHAT
YOU DON'T HAVE)

Chapter 10

Funding Models

I debated with myself about whether to include this chapter or not. On one hand, it is important for you to know your options for raising money to start or run your business, on the other I didn't want ⅓ of this book to be all about money. Ultimately, I realized that money is ever present and the more we can learn about it, the better.

Back when I was immersed in the world of tech, living and working in Silicon Beach, talking about, reading about and being informed about rounds of fundraising done by startups was normal and expected. I'd got out to lunch and catch glimpses of conversations between excited entrepreneurs and weary investors. Colleagues would approach my desk and ask me if I'd heard of the latest startup that raised several million dollars. But even though I was part of this world, I never even considered that I could pitch my idea to serious investors, much less actually have someone write me a check to start a business. The reason I never thought of it as an option even as people all around me were doing just that, was the simple fact that I didn't know I could. The only people I saw that were writing and also getting these checks, pretty much all looked the same and came from the same background. As of this writing about 78% of angel investors are male and 88% white. And since those investors overwhelmingly invest in "people like them", thinking of fundraising as a serious option for funding a startup can feel like an unlikely possibility. So because I never saw brown, immigrant, women selling their business idea, and getting people to invest in those ideas, my brain sort of made the assumption that if I wanted to start a business, the money would have to come from somewhere else.

It took me a while to undo this way of thinking and unfortunately it is still true that people like me have less of a chance of being funded by investors, but if there is one message I hope you take away from this and the last couple of chapters is that money truly is everywhere. If you start to allow yourself to think of it as something that serves a purpose, brings you joy and is easy to come by, then you can start to see all the options that are available to you when it comes to raising money to get your idea off the ground.

Self-Funding

The first and most obvious option is to fund your new venture yourself, otherwise known as bootstrapping. Using part of your current income, your savings, and asking friends and family for small investments all fall under self-funding. If you have already crunched the numbers and have seen that you won't need a huge amount to get started, then this could be a great option for you. Funding a business yourself gives you easy and fast access to money since, hey, it's your money already. And if you decide to pitch your idea to friends and family, and they agree to give small loans to help you get started, the terms and conditions for repayment, are usually pretty flexible. Best of all if you decide to self-fund, there is usually little to no paperwork involved since even if you do take money from family, a simple agreement or contract is often enough.

The downside to funding a business yourself is that it will eat away at your savings and if you have not prepared for that and have no other income coming in while you start your business, seeing that decline in your bank account month after month can be stressful to some, which means you will have to come up with solid mindset shifts to not let that get in your way. Also, if you do accept money from family and friends, you have to confront the possibility that this may cause a shift in the dynamic of the relationship and possibly cause some strain. But all in all, bootstrapping is great for small businesses who really only need a minimal initial boost to get things going.

Crowdfunding

At this point, platforms like Kickstarter have become a pretty ubiquitous fundraising option for innovative entrepreneurs. Unlike other forms of investment where you hope to get one big check, crowdfunding lets you get small donations from many people, who often become your first customers. This option essentially allows people to pay for your product before you actually produce it. When done right, crowdfunding generates a buzz around your product and serves as great early marketing. One of the biggest advantages about crowdfunding is that you get to connect with your early buyers, creating a perfect opportunity to do some market research with the people who, even without having seen your actual product or read any reviews, are wiling to buy it and support the manufacturing of it. Another huge advantage of a successful crowdfunding campaign is the possibility that it could attract other investors. There are many stories of viral crowdfunding campaigns that lead to outside investors pumping cash into a new business strictly because of the success of the campaign.

What you have to be aware of when it comes to crowdfunding is that it is a highly competitive field and it's not just because you put up a campaign that people will suddenly give you money. You will need good copywriting, great images, well-produced videos, and a very well thought-out and planned marketing strategy to boost traffic to your campaign, and attract the kind of person who wants what you have to offer, and is willing to pay for it before it has been produced.

Essentially for a crowdfunding campaign to be successful, it should be thought of as a business launch since a lot of the same planning has to go into it.

Angel Investors

If you are not familiar with Angel Investing, essentially it is a person or group of individuals who use their personal capital to invest in new businesses. The majority of Angels Investors are CEOs or former CEOs, so the major advantage is that you have a chance of being mentored by someone who is not only invested in your success but also has a lot of experience leading a successful company. The other advantage of this type of funding is that typically, Angel investors, are more likely to take a risk on innovative ideas. In fact, the majority of investment options rely less on the feasibility that your idea could be become a success and more on you. When you are the kind of person who can walk into a meeting with a potential investor and come across as passionate, knowledgeable about your field, with plenty of vision and guts, the idea itself often takes a backseat. And being that this kind of investing *is* so personal, it can be hard to find the right Angel investor. Not only that, this is also a highly competitive funding model, and ultimately is better for people who need a quick infusion of cash to get them started.

Venture Capitals

Unlike the options mentioned so far, seeking funding from a Venture Capital is a much more formal avenue of funding. These firms are managed by professional investors who are seeking big stake opportunities that have the potential to go public, so they can reap larger rewards and move on to other investments. This is a great option if you have already started or have the basics in place and are ready for rapid growth. Once a venture capital firm has agreed to invest, your business — from how you operate to your profits — will be closely watched and monitored. For most CEOs this is a good way to foster growth and sustainability since that amount of accountability can make people more motivated to perform at a higher level. And it is not just the accountability, VCs are also a great opportunity to get mentorship from highly regarded experts. However, most founders ultimately seek out this option because of the potential for big payouts for your company and its founders.

Ideally partnering with a VC should offer you a lot of leverage and support, but it is hard to predict just how much of that will be available to you. Depending on your particular deal, you can get as little as 3 years of support or as much as 10 years. You also lose a fair share of control since there are more people involved with different ideas of what constitutes success, and ultimately this option tends to be more attractive for those whose business have a higher potential for significant growth and high market share.

Accelerators

As the name indicates, accelerators are programs that help fast track the growth of your business. The main point of attraction is the amount of mentoring and guidance you get in an excellent program. That and becoming part of a community of other founders and startups who are at similar stages of growth to yours, can do a lot to keep you motivated and boost your sense of urgency. However, because the goal is to assist you with rapid growth, you will have a small window of support in which you have access to mentors and coaches. A lot of accelerators are also specialized, meaning they only accept certain kinds of businesses, and therefore acceptance is competitive. These kinds of programs can also be highly prohibitive for people with active home lives. Since you and your team have to operate out of a shared facility, often located in a major metropolitan hub, it can be hard for parents, caretakers, and those living in more remote locations to participate.

Contests and Prizes

As a founder being able to sell and explain your idea compellingly is a big part of your job, so competitions in which you pitch your idea for a chance at winning small amounts of capital, can be a quick win-win. You get to network with possible investors, other founders, potential new hires, while practicing the delivery of your idea and engaging in some early marketing. A lot of times, this can also be a good chance of getting some local media coverage which, again, serves as early marketing and could attract other investors. The downside here is that you have to practice, present and fail, a lot. If you have a sensitivity to rejection, and fear of public speaking, it will take some considerable amount of mental workout to become comfortable with both of these.

Loans and Microloans

It has become increasingly difficult to qualify for loans, yet banking institutions and microfinance providers can still be an option to explore when considering early funding. These institutions will analyze your idea and plan, and if they determine it to be a safe investment, you might have a chance at a loan. The obvious upside is that you get access to much-needed capital and if you have a good history with money and a good credit score, you might be able to get a considerable amount. However, banks do require a collateral so there is a risk of you losing your house, your car or any other valuable asset, should you fail to pay back your loan. And when it comes to micro lending, they are often predatory and you can be stuck paying a high interest on a small loan which may not be worth it in the long run.

Government Programs and Grants

The first step in applying for government programs or grants is research. Once you find the programs and grants for which your business could qualify, you will have to apply or prepare a proposal. From that point on, you will have to wait for an analysis to determine if you qualify, and only after everything is sorted, will you get access to the funds. There are so many programs available and a lot of times people have little to no knowledge of the incentives offered by governments, so depending on the category there could be little competition. This is an opportunity to get a significant amount of startup or growth capital from your local or national government. But as with anything that comes from the government, this is an option that requires you to go through a lot of bureaucracy. Not only that, the grant writing and application process can be very time-consuming and the time it takes them to respond can often be very slow, leaving you wondering if you will ever get the funds or not.

Credit Cards

I probably don't have to sell you on the advantages and disadvantages of using credit cards as an option to fund your business. Using your personal credit cards or taking credit in the name of your new organization are options available to you if you have relatively good credit history and the amounts will vary greatly from person to person depending on that history. The major advantage is that you have funds immediately available to help you get started, but the downside is that you have to start paying the debt back immediately and often credit cards, even for those with good credit can leave you paying high interest rates.

Pre-Sale

The idea behind a pre-sale is to start marketing and selling your product before it is ready to be delivered, so that you can fund the manufacturing or building of your product or service. The obvious upside is that you start to get paid before you have spent a lot, and essentially get your new customers to pay you to build your product. And because you have people who are willing to pay for something even before it is ready, you get to create a community of evangelist who will be your first reviewers and more likely to recommend your product or service to others. This is also a smart strategy to gauge interest and do more market research before you put the final touches on your product. Pre-selling may sound like a no-brainer, but you still need money and expertise to execute a pre-launch that attracts enough orders to justify the time and money spent on marketing a pre-launch.

As you can see, there are so many ways to raise, save, win, and get access to money to start your business, you just have to find the option that works best for where you are now. What you will see eventually is that money is everywhere. It just is. Just because it isn't in your account this very second, it doesn't mean that it won't be there next week. Of all the things that people who join the incubator list as a prohibitor, money is always the easiest to solve for.

I myself have gone the route of loans, credit cards, friends and family, and I have found that, for where I am in my business, bootstrapping and pre-selling has proved to be the best option. I now know myself enough to know that saving then spending gives me a better return. My business model is also one that works best when I build my products only after I have gotten significant feedback from my clients, so the quality of my products depends on pre-sale and market research.

That's not to say I discount any of the other options because if it weren't for loans, credit cards and friends and family, I wouldn't be at place where I have the luxury to opt for bootstrapping and pre-selling. So give yourself some time to analyze and research each and every option before deciding on what will work best for you. But as always, do not let this be something that paralyses you. Pick one, go for it full-heartedly and if it doesn't work, choose another route and keep going.

Metal Breakdown: I Can't Just Ask for Money Like That!

Asking can be such a triggering task. The idea that you need to ask for money in the first place can be humiliating and bring forth all kinds of feelings of unworthiness. It is hard enough to put your idea out there, now add begging for money to the list and it can be enough to make you want to quit the whole thing right now.

I remember setting up a Kickstarter campaign for my manufacturing business and looking back now, there was so much that I didn't know, but I went for it in the best way I could. I spent hours writing the copy, producing a video, setting up the page... When it came time to email all my friends and family, I could feel the embarrassment rising in me before I clicked send on what I saw as me shamelessly begging for money. Instead of being proud of the work I had done and feeling like people should want to invest in my idea because it had the potential to be something great, all I could do is feel embarrassed, and wonder what my friends would think of me and how they would judge me. I felt they would judge my idea, my product, my asking for money, but even through all that shame and fear, I still clicked "send" on the email announcing my campaign. What followed was a show of support that I was definitely not expecting. People who I had not heard from in ages, donated and left encouraging words, wishing me the best.

That campaign was not a success, and we only got about half of what we had hoped for. It was yet another experience that left me feeling like a failure, reinforcing negative thoughts I already had about myself, again. But after the period of mourning that I always go through after a major set back, I do the only thing I know, which is sit down, write, and figure out what to do next.

The thing is that you either allow your idea become a business or you let a solvable thing like lack of money become your mantra and excuse for not moving forward. You have to look at the prospect of starting something on your own as a nonnegotiable. Also, I am firm believer in pressure. A lot of times when we are put against a wall, we always find ways to make things work. So find that sense of urgency in you and put your ass to work on the getting the money. After all, you have something amazing to offer the world and you can't let a little thing like money, get in your way.

PERMISSION SLIP:

MONEY IS A SOLVABLE PROBLEM. GO OUT AND GET IT!

Chapter 11

Your MVP

O f all the things I wish I had known before starting a business, understanding a minimum viable product (MVP) and how it is meant to serve a new business is at the top of the list.

What is an MVP?

Your MVP is essentially a simplified version of your product and service that you will use as a test in the initial phase of your business. It is the first version of your idea that will serve to get your business off the ground. And while an MVP is unique to each business, and I can't give you an example that will exactly fit what *you* have in mind, the basic thinking behind conceptualizing and creating a minimum viable product will be the same no matter what the business.

Your minimum viable product, essentially, is a bare-bones, basic version of your idea. For a lot of people not familiar with this concept, it can sound contradictory to start with something that does not feel like a finished product. Some people — ahem, perfectionists — have a hard time with the idea of starting with something that isn't exactly what they have in mind. While that makes sense in theory, in practice you want to avoid spending a ton of time and money on developing something "perfect," and instead start with something that is as basic as possible without compromising the quality, usability, or reputation of your young brand. You want to make sure you are creating something that will attract your first customers, without wasting valuable time, money, and energy building something that you're not yet sure is what your ideal customers want.

MVP for Software-Based Businesses

If you have an idea for a killer app that will change the world, before you spend a ton of cash and hundreds of hours building a complete version, break it down to the essentials by asking yourself: what is the single most important thing this app needs to have and do? You want to find the essence of your application, the one function it needs to accomplish to give people a clear idea of how you will solve their problem. A good example is Instagram. Think of all the things you can do on Instagram today: Share photos, add captions, "like," mute, block, search, use hashtags, add stories, embellish those stories, add to your highlights, track your analytics, and so on. But back when it first launched it was a simple photo-sharing service. Period. That was enough for its founders to get an idea if people even had an interest in sharing photos in that format, outside of other social media platforms like Facebook, which hadn't been done at the time. They knew that testing that initial concept was the first step in validating their idea, and starting with something that did too much more than that would have been too big a learning curve for their users and not worth the time and effort. So if you are building your app, consider a similar path.

MVP for Service-Based Businesses

As someone who was about to launch a service-based business, the question I had to answer was "What is the one thing I want people to take away from joining this incubator and hiring me as a business coach?" For me, it was really important to help as many people as possible in any part of the world, and guarantee that each new founder had the guidance needed to transform themselves from a person filled with insecurities to someone with the confidence to continue on their entrepreneurship journey. Those were my top three priorities, so when it came to launching the first version of the incubator with my first cohort of founders, anything that took away from that goal was seen as an extra. All the nice things people see and have when they join today were not part of my MVP. I didn't have any professional videos (actually I had no videos at all; I created videos later based on the feedback from my initial founders), I did not have a professional website, nor a membership hosting platform, consistent branding, or even an official name or logo. All I had was a welcome email, a Zoom account where I could host my coaching sessions, and a Facebook group where I could go to answer questions. That was it. And it was enough.

If you are planning a service-based business, figure out what is essential to your offerings and focus on providing the best service you can without letting the "extras" or "nice to haves" distract you.

MVP for Product-Based Businesses

For most, a product-based business is the easiest to break down to basics in order to create your first version. Just as you can break down a digital application to its basic function, you want to create a prototype that performs the main function of your product. But one question I often get is what if I have an idea for a product-based business that needs to have lots of products at once, like a makeup or skincare line, or a fashion business? My answer is this: Just because you see more established brands launching 60 products in one collection, by no means is that what you have to do. I worked with a founder who had a million and one ideas for her vegan, toxic-free, makeup and skincare line for teens, and who was having a hard time conceptualizing her MVP. In a case like this, the best course of action is to first survey your ideal customers and find out what kinds of products they are more likely to purchase. Once you have that, survey what variations they would most like to see. In her case, she asked them what shades and scents they wanted to see the most or were more likely to purchase. By following this process she was able to narrow down her MVP to a simple starter collection of three shades of lip gloss, making it a simple yet powerful way to introduce herself to a new market where she was still learning and making a name for herself. Your focus should be on creating and selling, and only when you have an understanding of what your customer wants, add more to your line.

I Have an MVP, Now What?

The number one function of a minimum viable product is to educate both you and your customer. Once you create your MVP, you will launch your product, and after that, gauge the response. Essentially, you will set in motion a cycle that will be your guarantee to consistent, sustainable growth.

After your MVP launch, your goal is to gather as much information as you can. How are your first clients using your product or service? What do they like about it? What do they think could improve? What is a feature or product that is not being used or selling well? Why? The beauty of this process is that from here on out, you can let your customers be your guide. There will be no guessing or shooting in the dark, hoping that the next improvement will be something your clients will respond well to. Every addition or shift will come from an educated place, making it more likely that your existing customers will stick around, make a return purchase, or better yet, recommend you to their friends.

You can see this cycle of launch, gather information, improve, repeat, in your favorite businesses. Let's go back to Instagram. Once they had loyal (or even addicted) users, it became easy to add and try out new features based on feedback. Videos, stories, tagging, adding location, and Instagram TV are all features created through direct learning from how people were interacting with the app, or leaving the app to interact with a competitor. As of this writing, the latest improvement was taking away the feature that lets you see how many "likes" an image has. As much as some people hated to see that feature go, Instagram knew that ultimately it would be a success based on feedback, social pressure, and conversations with their loyal user base.

In my case, the way this cycle plays out is this: Through customer surveys and analytics, I learn what pre-recorded content the founders in my incubator are getting the most useful information from and which videos they skip, which tells me where I need to add more information, what I need to clarify, and what I can cut out. Through my live interactions with the founders, I learn the most common obstacles, which again, guides my content and tells me what I can use in my marketing. I also hear from my clients about what improvements they want to see in terms of production value and design, and the format that best works for them, making it easier for me to know where I need to focus my efforts and resources. You will find that rather than spending forever trying to make the "perfect" thing, letting your customers do the work for you is not only smarter, but way more fun, too. There is nothing like seeing people excited to help you improve your product.

The secret here is to test quickly, learn quickly, and improve quickly. One mistake I see a lot of founders make is testing until they get the result they want. If there is a feature or a product you felt should work or sell well, but ends up not performing as you had hoped, move on. Remember, you are creating something for your ideal customer, not trying to change your customer's mind about what they should like.

Mental Breakdown: Fear of Criticism and Feedback

"But I have a vision... I know exactly what I want!" Whenever I hear this from a founder, I translate that as, "I have an idea, but I am afraid that if I let people see it before it's perfect, they'll tell me they don't like it, and I don't want to feel like I am not good enough."

Listen, I am still so afraid of criticism that I find myself shrieking in response to my life partner trying to give me feedback on basically anything. Just today, we were riding bikes, and he pointed out that I should make an adjustment to my gears because they were clearly grinding, and needed a shift. So when he said, "Hey, you need to change your gears," what I heard was, "You don't know what you're doing. You're doing something wrong." Crazy, but totally normal.

In my business, it was criticism and negative feedback that made me completely change the way I do my videos. Truly being open to criticism and feedback improved how people interacted with my content, which improved people's performance, which resulted in better testimonials, which brought me more clients. If I hadn't asked for feedback, and discovered that people thought my initial content was kind of boring and long, I wouldn't have changed it, and my business would certainly not be where it is today.

We are something like 5 times more likely to remember a negative comment or experience than a good one, so it makes sense that we would like to avoid situations that put us directly in the line of fire for receiving feedback, negative or not. And while I can't help you see your mother's, your spouse's, or your frenemy's advice as a growth opportunity, when it comes to your business, feedback does equal growth, and growth means success for your business. So I suggest you start to see the feedback from your customers not as criticisms of you, or even your product, but as keys to the success of your business. Each time you see the same criticism over and over in surveys or reviews, it is the universe's way of pointing your focus in the direction of success.

PERMISSION SLIP:

YOU CAN SEE CRITICISM AS AN OPPORTUNITY FOR GROWTH

Chapter 12

Ready to Launch

After months of research, lining up businesses and mental health experts, setting up needed tech tools, and finalizing my business model, I finally had my MVP. I knew how the incubator would run in its first iteration, and I was ready to open applications for our first cohort of founders. And that's when the work really started.

Deciding what your business will do, who you will partner with, who you will sell to, and building an MVP are the low risk aspects of a business. Figuring out when and how you will find your first customers, or creating a launch plan, are when you face the fact that if you want to be an entrepreneur, your business actually has to, well — do business.

Part of me, when writing this book, wanted to talk about marketing strategies, launch timelines, campaign budgets, and all the specifics people usually consider when they think of a launch plan. But then I looked at my own launch and realized that I didn't follow any of the rules of a traditional launch. That worked for me. Like all the tips I give you in the book, I don't want you to go out there and robotically follow what has worked for someone else. It is your business, and you have the freedom to launch in whatever way feels authentic to you. The most I can offer you is guidance, inspire you to do your own research, and encourage you to figure out what will work for you where you are now. I cannot assume you have a budget, want to place ads, or have the means to hire a designer. But I can give you a roadmap so that you know where to begin and where the finish line is.

#businessgoals

A good place to start is identifying where you would like to end up. People are either driven by goals or prefer a fluid approach to life. Regardless of how you identify, there needs to be room for you to define what will make your launch successful. Setting a specific goal will help you keep track of your benchmarks, so that with each improvement of your product, you can clearly identify your areas of growth.

There are so many ways to gauge a successful launch, and you get to decide what those will be for your new business. Depending on your business, you may want to set your goals around getting good publicity, determining the number of new clients you will sign up, identifying the number items you will sell, or a percentage of growth you hope to see.

I am never one to discourage lofty goals, but if this is your first time launching the first version of your product, being conservative might serve you better in the long run. This strategy gives you the opportunity to really engage with your new audience, build a relationship, and learn from them. When I launched the incubator, my goal was to accept three founders into the program. That's it. For me, three people would be enough to test any tech kinks that would inevitably need to be worked out, without having to enlist a lot of outside help should something massive go wrong. It let me test out the group coaching format, and how I could best serve multiple people in one session. It also meant that I could give them my full attention as they progressed through the do-it-yourself parts of the program, and quickly make improvements. By keeping things small, I also created a sense of ownership in those first members. I was open and honest with them, and created a culture of feedback that encouraged them to be open with me about areas where the program needed improvement.

For you, a conservative goal might be a smaller number of sales so you can quality-test your first product run and make sure your shipping process is running smoothly. Perhaps you already had a launch that didn't go well, and now you want to set a small goal to test your new strategies. Or maybe you are hoping your messaging creates a viral event, and you're curious to see what the public's reaction will be. Again, this is *your* business, "success" can be whatever you want it to be.

Your Audience

If you have yet to clearly define your ideal customer, this is the time to do it. If you've done surveys and validated your idea, you should have some clue as to who your customers are, their values, where they hang out, and what kind of language connects with them. Knowing their age, the gender they identify with, their location, their spending power or income, job titles, and hobbies and interests, makes it a lot easier to provide them with valuable information so they can more easily connect with you and your brand.

Don't be afraid to really narrow things down. For me, I knew that I wanted to reach out to people who identified as mothers with not much time to spare, who lacked knowledge or experience starting a business, and who also had a lot of insecurities around entrepreneurship. But just because I was targeting a specific type of person, it didn't mean they were the only people who connected with my messaging and approach. A lot of people who were not mothers still felt a connection with what I had to offer because they identified with having little time. Some recognized that even though they had the time, they had a lot of doubts and insecurities. Others had the knowledge, but didn't know how to manage their time or hold themselves accountable. By narrowing it down, you actually open space for people to see themselves in different aspects of your messaging and brand.

Talk the Talk

I encourage you to find freedom and wiggle room in every bit of advice I give you in this book, but one thing I feel you owe to your future customers and to your business is identifying with at least one aspect of your ideal customer. It is so much more enjoyable doing business with people you understand. Truly understanding the impact that solving a problem will have in someone else's life is a powerful motivator.

You may have noticed that over the past few years even enormous brands no longer operate as faceless organizations. From cheeky Twitter accounts that make you feel like there really is a person behind a brand, to celebrity CEOs, many businesses today tap into our craving for real human connection. We want to know the "personality" of the businesses we love. We are becoming more conscious and accepting of the fact that where we shop and who we support is a vote for that brand's values and virtues.

This is why you, my dear business founder, are marketing gold! You have an incredible power to persuade, help, and lead people. Just by being who you are, and becoming the face of your organization, you can help people understand what your business is about, why what you are doing matters, and why your ideal clients should trust you enough to buy what you have to offer, join your club, hire your services, or take the time to learn about what you are doing.

The key to harnessing this incredible power is authenticity. And this is the reason it is so important that you identify with your ideal clients in some way. You want to be able to speak to them from a place of truth. I admit that in the beginning this can be a bit of a challenge, but when you share your fears, you are touching on their fears, and when you talk about your wins, they are wins your customers are also seeking.

I readily admit that I find very little joy in social media. It is natural for me to leave the house without my phone, I do not check or "like" my friends posts often, and I can go weeks without taking a single picture of my adorable toddler, much less myself. So for me, this part of my business definitely started as a "must do" rather than "want to do" and it took a lot of meditation and conscious effort on my part to find and pleasure in it. But I knew that if I didn't put myself out there and let my future clients know that I was also a mom, someone who tried and failed a lot, had insecurities, and cared about the injustices they were facing because I had faced them too, I would never gain their trust, which is the first step in gaining their business.

My process of transformation started slowly. Because I was very private, and fearful of exposure, I first had to find the channel that would work for me. So I did a bit of a tour of all the major social media platforms, making mental lists of the things I felt could work for me and those that felt outside my comfort zone. I eventually landed on Instagram because I inherently have a love for photography, so knew I would enjoy that aspect. I also knew that only a small percentage of people actually read captions, so people who took the time to read through my long posts would actually connect with what I had to say.

This process of finding and owning your personal voice, specifically when it comes to your business, is a journey unto itself. One of my favorite things is to witness the growth of a founder after they've gone through this process. I have seen so many women go from struggling to be comfortable with who they are to realizing the power of their personality and perspective. I have seen timid people who never talk about themselves transform into passionate founders who beam with excitement when they finally find the medium to share who they are, allowing them to truly connect with their first customers.

Rules of Social Media

More and more it is becoming apparent that popularity does not translate into dollars, so before you start thinking that being active and comfortable on social media is all you have to do to bring success to your brand, let me make a few things clear. *Consistency* is a lot more important than frequency. Just because you post nineteen times a day, it does not mean you will find your people more quickly. I post on social media every other month, but I email my audience weekly and it is more than enough to stay connected.

Quality is better than quantity. Who cares if you have a million followers. If those people are not engaging with your content, liking, commenting, or sending you messages, you are not making meaningful connections. Your goal is to find people who are more likely to purchase from you, not find the most people. I have barely 5,000 followers but I hear from them constantly, have formed amazing friendships, and many of them eventually joined the incubator.

Content is king. Your perfect picture does not matter. What you have to say, does. I keep repeating this because it's true. You want to connect with your ideal customers, so sharing your story, motivation, values, inspirations, and tips has to be a natural part of that. The best part about owning your story and sharing it is that you can speak with complete authority on the matter.

You and Your Content

Deciding what you will share, and determining whether is has value, will come from experience and how your audience reacts. There is a simple process that will likely yield good results, however: share what scares.

This concept is not about being fearless; being vulnerable is always scary. It is about knowing that fear can be a common point of connection between you and your ideal customers. Your pain point is their pain point. The beautiful things is that you have a solution for them: your product or service.

Before you start posting your whole life story, here is a bit of guidance on editing. You want to tell a story and paint a picture with your words. Next, you will decide if you will place ads or grow organically, but this strategy applies either way. Take a look at this post:

Notice how I start by placing my reader in a scene? I was nursing, taking a phone call, and looking at my partner. Once my reader is there, then I tell them what I was thinking and why it matters. This post served a few purposes and used an arc that I follow pretty much every time I write a post for social media, which helps gauge whether my audience can identify with a particular pain point (in this case having to do multiple things at once). I was able to introduce my purpose, share my solution, and give my ideal customers a call to action to connect with me.

So even if you don't write a lot and have some fears about your current abilities, don't worry. Not all my posts are winners even for people who have been doing this for a while. But you will get it right more often than not the more you practice. My advice is that you start by following the arch above and branch out when you start to feel more confident (and if you have the time, do a bit of studying on the art of copywriting). So again, my basic arc for copywriting is this: paint a picture, introduce the pain point, share the solution and how it differs from what's out there, and create a call to action.

Ad or Not, Here You Come!

Before I move ahead, let's recap where you are at this point in your launch plan. So far you have:

1. Set your end goal.
2. Identified your target audience.
3. Developed an understanding of the role your story will play in marketing.
4. Decided what channel works best for you.
5. Developed a basic understanding of how to write effective copy.

Now it is time to decide if you want to set a budget and create an ad campaign, or take your time and grow your business and your following organically by personally reaching out to ideal future clients.

If you decide to place ads, the first thing you want to do is set a budget. It's so easy to let things run on autopilot, trying to get just a few more eyes on your ads. But the next thing you know you've spent US$4,000 and have nothing to show for it (yup, I did that). Setting a small budget lets you test quickly, gauge your results quickly, and decide the best course of action quickly — which we love.

The next step is to decide where you will be placing these ads so you can design your ad and write your copy. Please don't go crazy here by spending money you should be saving. I am not lying when I say that simple is better. Just take a look at my best performing ad after over 6 months of testing with a team of experts.

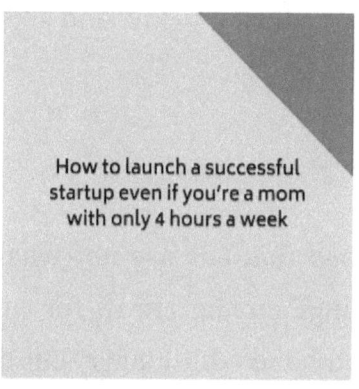

How to launch a successful startup even if you're a mom with only 4 hours a week

You can't get simpler than that. The juicy bit was in the copy where I told my story and connected with my future clients via text, giving them a reason to click and learn more. Like I have said before, the copy can follow the same arc as your social media posts, but I do recommend you spend some time doing a bit of research on effective copywriting. When in doubt, I always look to those who are 10 steps ahead of me so I don't waste time reinventing the wheel. There are countless books, blogs, and video tutorials that can help you polish skills you are still developing.

The only thing left after you have finished creating your ad is to go live — yay! —and monitor your campaigns. It is in the monitoring phase that you will learn what is working and what needs to be adjusted. Let's repeat it once more so it sticks: test quickly, learn quickly, adjust quickly. And good luck!

Ads Not for You

Now if you decided that ads are not where you are just yet, and want to do things on the cheap for now (which I highly encourage), then you have a bit longer, but ultimately more fun road ahead.

A lot of people still ask if it really is possible to launch without an ad budget, and I undoubtedly say yes, it is. All it takes is a bit of time and networking. I started the incubator, knowing I wanted to find and build relationships with my first founders before accepting them into the program. In fact, there are a lot of scenarios where advertising would not be the right course of action. If you are planning a business where you will be selling your items to larger retailers (wholesale), then networking will be where your first sales more than likely come from.

Some people visibly cringe at the thought of networking. But trust me, there are so many ways to network today. Even if you hate leaving the house, you can still build a solid group of contacts. Again, regardless of how you choose to start, you want to make up your mind to network with a purpose, not just get the most contacts. You want to connect with people who you can genuinely help, or who have expressed an interest in helping you. Never *ever* network with selling in mind. Someone who clearly only wants to make a sale is no fun for anyone.

If you love people and can't wait to get out of the house, I recommend you find a calendar of events for your area and add any and all events that fit your industry or vibe to your personal calendar. If you have the time and means, then go ahead, get dressed, get out of the house, and start making a name for yourself. Like I already mentioned, networking is as much about giving as it is receiving, so always have something to offer when you have something to ask.

Let's say you meet another founder who is in a similar market and you want to know the secrets to her success. You can't just ask her to meet for coffee and "pick her brain" (please do not use that phrase). Ask her about where she is struggling and could use some help. She might have an open position that she just can't fill, but you have a cousin who would be perfect for the role. Bam! You just created a win, win, win situation. Don't be afraid to take your time. Get to know people, reach out to your new contacts periodically, take a genuine interest in them, form a relationship, and then try to explore how you can benefit.

If online networking is more your speed, the same rules apply, except you have an endless list of possible networking venues. The main difference between real life networking and going online is the fact that people at a networking event are expecting a particular type of connection to be formed, whereas when you reach out to people online, you are probably interrupting them in the middle of something, and they then have to make the choice to interact with you. The trick is to create a template to get the conversation started.

When I first started reaching out to people to let them know about the incubator, I would search people by hashtags, check out their profiles, and if it seemed like I could help them, reach out with a simple message. I would introduce myself, share a bit about my story (naming my old pain points), and ask their permission to share more if they identified with my journey. If I got a negative response, then no hard feelings, I wished them luck and encouraged to reach out if they ever felt the need.

When I got a positive response, I would start a conversation that eventually led to asking them to have a phone chat with me. Then and only then, and again, only after asking permission, I would share that I had just launched an incubator for mothers and women because of my passion for seeing underrepresented people gain confidence while starting a business. A lot of these chats led to nothing, some led to people joining the program, and others led to long-term friendships. Some of my biggest paychecks have come through the connections I made with people I met via direct message on social media. These people turned into evangelists for what I do because of the friendship or mentorship I had taken the time to nurture.

Launch 1.0 and Beyond

Reader, I have both good news and fun news. The good news is that you are now ready to launch! The fun news is that this is just the beginning of your entrepreneur journey.

If your initial launch is a big success, and you've reached your goal, yay! Go out, do something fun, splurge on something, whatever. I am a huge fan of massages as a reward because it actually gives me time and space to think about what I have just accomplished. Once you are done celebrating, the next step is to study your launch strategy. You want to understand what made it successful so you can replicate it, build on it, and use your learnings as a model for future growth.

If you did not reach your goal, it is also important that you allot time to nurture yourself. I still need at least a few days after every major setback to get myself ready to move on to the next thing. Even after all this time, and all the work I have done, it is still a challenge to not personalize failure, so that time of meditation, reflection, and therapy is crucial. By now I've hit so many bumps in my business journey, however, that I have learned to manage them in a way that feels healthy for me. So I treat failure as just another phase in the process, and just as I budget time for everything else in my business, I now also budget time for wallowing in self-pity. Depending on the size of the disappointment, I allow myself anywhere from an hour to a couple of weeks of recovery time. And in that time, I really let myself go through all the emotions needed to get me through this difficult phase. I also comfort myself by doing things that let me quiet the negative self-talk. I eat comfort foods, I binge on a favorite show, go out for drinks, and don't let myself feel guilty about it. After all, I am in mourning.

Once my pity party has lost its glamour and I feel ready to brush it all off, I really get the ball rolling. I clean myself up, I reorganize my work space, and I tap into the side of me that feels encouraged by the prospect of starting over. Now is the time to study your efforts and find the lessons: was it a marketing issue, an audience issue, a product issue? Figure that shit out, create a new plan, and keep going. Always.

Mental Breakdown: Imposter Syndrome

So we finally get to the granddaddy of entrepreneurial insecurities. Imposter syndrome is a nasty bugger likely to hit just as you are about to do something amazing. It does not discriminate, and it is loud. You know the wave is hitting you when start to feel like a fraud, inadequate, not meant to be where you are, or doing what you are doing. The crazy thing is that you will feel this even when you have plenty of evidence to the contrary, even when you have people praising you, even when you are an authority in your field.

I still get a flick to the ear from imposter syndrome every time I welcome a new founder to the incubator. I still think I don't know enough to guide people through the process of launching a business, I am not well-adjusted enough to help people gain confidence in themselves, I am not white enough to get people to trust me. I still have to shake that feeling off and yell "that's just bullshit, and I'm not buying it!"

Dear founder, you will feel it too. It's part of the process. We are so used to being labeled as one thing and not another that when we strive to create new versions of ourselves and adopt new identities, imposter syndrome is there to try to put us back in our lane. We also spend so much time trying not to fail that the mere thought of being exposed can make us feel like an imposter. And when it comes for you, I want you to be ready to defend your self.

First, allow yourself to feel it. You've got to be able to name it in order to conquer it. These thoughts come from patterns formed long ago, so it is inevitable that you will feel its seductive power trying to drag you to a place you no longer belong. Then, find help, because it's hard to be your own cheerleader all the time. This journey is already a roller coaster, and having someone there who can be honest with you, who can identify with you, and who can show you all the evidence that you deserve to feel good about yourself no matter your past will help you feel less alone.

Beyond that, you have to find the lessons, the path to growth from where you are. One of my favorite quotes is "If I knew better, I would have done better." We are all just using the tools we have available to us at the time, so try to find a new tool, a new learning experience, each time you feel like you have failed. But most of all, be kind and gentle with yourself. You are allowed to make mistakes, you are allowed to learn, you are allowed to grow.

You are also allowed to succeed. You are allowed to celebrate your accomplishments. You are allowed to visualize a better version of yourself and work to make it a reality, no matter how many times you stumble.

PERMISSION SLIP:

NO MATTER
WHAT, YOU CAN
BE A SUCCESSFUL
ENTREPRENEUR

In Conclusion

My fellow founder, I want to thank you for making it this far and for trusting me to take you on this journey.

As I mentioned in the introduction, this book is by no means to be used as a guide where every step must be taken lock step. This book is about information. It is a collection of things I wish I had known about when I started my first business.

Ultimately, I want you to think of this book as a love letter to people who have big ideas, but have always felt less than. I hope I have given you the tools to wiggle your way out of the chains of fear, insecurity and doubt so you can unleash the powerful entrepreneur within you and bring your ideas to the world.

With love,

Nas

PS: If you need extra support, or are curious about how you can join the Perfect Startup Incubator where we can meet live so I can help you launch your business while letting go of your insecurities, you can reach me directly at nas@theminddesigner.com.

Acknowledgments

I would like to start by thanking my mother, Etna, for being a constant source of support throughout the many bumps in my entrepreneurial path, my life partner, Alex and our son who are always there to remind me how good we have it, my editor, Wendy, for making this the smoothest rookie effort and helping me feel like I could actually pull this writing thing off. I am so grateful for all the members of Perfect Startup Incubator for showing me what true grit, perseverance and resilience looks like. Lastly, I have to acknowledge all the coaches I've had throughout my life for helping me build the steps on my growth ladder.